How to Get Started in Writing

How to
Get
Started
in
Writing

by
Peggy Teeters

Writer's
Digest
Books

Cincinnati, Ohio

Second printing 1982.
First paperback printing, 1986.
Second paperback printing, 1987.

Library of Congress Cataloging in Publication Data

Teeters, Peggy. 1918—
   How to get started in writing.

   Bibliography: p.
   Includes index.
   1. Authorship. I. Title.
PN147.T33   808'.02   81-14632
ISBN 0-89879-239-8   AACR2

The permissions acknowledgments on the two following pages constitute an extension of this copyright page.

Permissions Acknowledgments

To my children,
and to the memory of my mother

Acknowledgments

*I'd like to thank the following for their
help in writing the book:
Carol Cartaino, Howard I. Wells III, Patrick J. O'Connor
Judy Boesch, Carol Jenkins, Dody Smith
my students in the "Write Now!" classes*

Contents

uscript. Keeping a carbon. What about SASE? Mail out more than one. Looking for the right market. Study the format of the publication. How to address the envelope.

market. The fiction market. The book market. Markets for nostalgia.

phy. Keeping a diary or a journal. Collect stories on tape now. The Encyclopedia of American Facts. Reading *Who Do You Think You Are*. A local man writes about Maryland history. A military man compiles material about World War II. Start a diary or journal now.

1

Don't Wait to Communicate

Get ready to enter the world of Shakespeare, Shelley, Byron, Keats, Milton, Dante, Dickens, Stevenson, Eliot, the Brownings, Dickinson, Frost, and the many other writers of the past. These men and women left a legacy for mankind to cherish and enjoy. But the writers of today are also contributing to that special gift, and it isn't too late for you to join them. Decide right now to use your creative powers and learn how to become a writer. There's no doubt about it—you can do it!

If it's been years since you read the works of these literary giants, this is the time to browse at your library and become immersed in genius. But as you reread *Hamlet* or "Ode to the West Wind," go one step further. Do some research on the lives of these writers and jot down some of the details. You'll find that these people experienced the problems we all encounter in our daily lives. Eventually, your notes will add up to a feature article or some interesting fillers that point out some of their human frailties.

For example, you'll discover that John Keats knew only too well that feeling of life slipping by too quickly. All of us, whether we are twenty or sixty, experience that sensation now and then, and wish we could stop the hands of time. Keats especially was overwhelmed by the thought that he could never finish what he had set out to accomplish. One of his poems begins:

> When I have fears that I may cease to be
> Before my pen has gleaned my teeming brain . . .

It's possible that he had a premonition about an early death; he was only twenty-five when he died from tuberculosis. But in that short time, he managed to write some of the purest poetry in any literature and carved a niche for himself in the field of English Romanticism. And who can help but be inspired by this line from one of his poems: "A thing of beauty is a joy forever"?

As you rub elbows if only briefly with writers of the past and present, ask yourself what characteristics apply to all of them. You'll soon come to the conclusion that communicativeness heads the list; they all had the desire to share their innermost thoughts and feelings with the world. Isn't this your dream too? Here then is your link to those creative men and women you so much admire. But writers of all ages are also versatile, moody, absentminded, sensitive, individualistic, persevering, determined, and enthusiastic. Add a sense of humor to that list of adjectives, and you'll have the definition of someone who is a professional writer—or destined to be. If you take a good, honest look at yourself, you'll see that this description comes close to qualifying you for the job of becoming a wordsmith.

Are you worried because you already know that you can only write on a part-time basis? Chase all your fears away. William Faulkner wrote *Sanctuary* in the boiler room of a power plant where he worked for one year. Phyllis Wheatley worked on her book of poetry whenever her duties as a slave allowed her a moment or two. Jane Austen scribbled notes for her novels in the midst of family conversations. Maya Angelou dredged up memories of her childhood even while she danced and sang and traveled and finally produced a remarkable autobiography, *I Know Why the Caged Bird Sings*. Anthony Trollope worked in a post office for years but wrote his classic Victorian novels before dawn or on his way to work. His mother, Frances Trollope, started her writing career at fifty and turned out 114 books, mainly novels and stories of her travels.

Creativity seems to flourish at any age with the proper nourishment. During the past five years, teachers in the elementary and junior high schools have experimented with creative writing workshops held after class. They have been amazed at the response and the results. They found that their students were able to sell their poems, articles, and stories to well-known juvenile magazines. What also surprised them was the fact that more than twenty editors are looking for young writers to send in their material and receive their first byline. (Some of these magazines also pay their contributors.)

On the older level, several publications are now running writing contests for young adults. The winners not only get their names in print but also receive a tidy sum of money. What is even more newsworthy is the sudden interest in the fiction field. The beginning writer now has a chance to become the storyteller he's always wanted to be and challenge the professional. This is the time to learn how to do it.

But do the creative juices still flow when an individual reaches the "golden years"? According to the experts, they never dry up, and these experts maintain that the creative process can actually add years to your life. It brings out positive and constructive attitudes in you and results in your turning out remarkable works of art or handicrafts or literary endeavors. Many older men and women have already won acclaim; Pablo Casals played the cello and conducted orchestras up to the time of his death at ninety-six; Grandma Moses took up painting at the age of seventy-seven; Carl Sandburg wrote his six-volume biography of Lincoln when he was in his sixties and seventies; and Agatha Christie came up with another whodunit when she was eighty.

But what about the unknowns? Do they stand a chance against the established writers? They certainly do. Dr. James Herriot didn't dream that his homespun stories about his experiences as a veterinarian in Yorkshire, England, would win him fame and fortune. Stephen King didn't know when he quit his job as an English teacher to devote all of his time to writing that his horror novels would meet with great success. Maxine Hong Kingston was more than surprised when her memoirs, *The Woman Warrior*, received high praise from the American community as well as the Chinese. Mary Ellen Pinkham didn't have an inkling that her collection of household hints would become a top-ten bestseller. Richard Nelson Boles didn't expect to see his book *What Color is Your Parachute?* become a guide in many career courses. Richard Simmons, that youthful TV personality, wasn't quite prepared for the success of his *Never-Say-Diet Book*.

Robert Fontaine, a humorist who has written hundreds of lighthearted pieces for the *Saturday Evening Post* and other periodicals, wrote the following words in *The Writer's Handbook* for the beginning writer:

> To be a writer is something special. It is to reach, however awkwardly, for the stars and to move, however haltingly, in that direction. To be a beginner or a semiprofessional or a part-time writer is something just as special as to be a hardened professional.
>
> It's time to reach for the stars!

If this quote has inspired you once and for all to fulfill your ambition to become a writer, don't lose your momentum. Read this guide and learn how to fan that flame of creativity you've had burning for such a long time. This book was written for all of you who have often wished to find guidelines that could show you how to get started in fiction or nonfiction, guidelines that were easy to follow and yet informative.

In these chapters you will learn how to choose a subject, how to research it, and how to develop it into a professional manuscript. You'll discover how to create a story from what you see and hear all around you, and how to make your characters, plot, and dialogue all fit into the mosaic of a good story. You'll find that with a little know-how you can become a columnist for a local newspaper and then try your wings with one of the syndicates. You'll see it's even possible for a beginner to do a children's story or write a book or write his memoirs.

As you read this handbook on writing, be aware of one important fact: the author became a professional writer even though she moved more than twenty-five times in twenty years and raised five children. If I accomplished my goal on a part-time basis, so can you!

2

Stop! Look! Listen!

You've made the decision and you're all set to become a writer. But where will you find the ideas? If you sharpen your five senses, you'll soon have a gold mine that will supply you with writing material for years to come.

You probably think you are quite observant. Are you? Whose picture is on the $5 bill? The $10 bill? How many tines are there on a fork? How many columns are in the portico of the White House? What four words appear on every U.S. coin? What kind of trees are in front of your house? Don't despair if you are groping around for the answers. Most of us don't pay enough attention to the world around us. But now that you are planning to become a writer, take time not only to smell the roses but also to notice their color and texture and shape.

Using their powers of observation, many renowned writers were able to paint word pictures for their readers. In this excerpt from *Look Homeward, Angel* (Charles Scribner's Sons, 1929) Thomas Wolfe uses sensory words that make us feel that we are actually at the table with Eugene Gant's family, relishing every bite:

> At the mid-day meal, they ate heavily: a huge pot roast of beef, fat buttered lima-beans, tender corn smoking on the cob, thick red slabs of sliced tomatoes, rough savory spinach, hot yellow cornbread, flaky biscuits, a deep-dish peach and apple cobbler spiced with cinnamon. . .

In the same novel, the author also makes us use our sense of smell when he writes:

> [He remembered the smell of] crushed mint leaves and of a wet lilac bush; of magnolia beneath the heavy moon; of dogwood and laurel; of an old caked pipe and Bourbon rye, aged in kegs of charred oak; the sharp smell of tobacco; of carbolic and nitric acids, the coarse true smell of a dog; of old imprisoned books; and the cool fern smell near springs; of vanilla in cake-dough; and of cloven ponderous cheeses.

Robert Louis Stevenson is another writer who painted word pictures. Find a copy of *Treasure Island* or *Travels with a Donkey* or *Kidnapped* and discover for yourself his ability to observe and describe. Read some of Ernest Hemingway's stories and see how even in his laconic and direct style he can still make the reader feel he is part of the action. In his famous short story, "Big Two-Hearted River," his use of sensory words makes it possible for everyone to experience Nick Adams's fishing trip: we can smell the coffee brewing; taste the buckwheat cakes; feel the river current against our legs and the pull of the trout on the line; and enjoy the serenity of nature.

Joan Mills, a housewife from New England, has always been interested in this style of writing, and when she moved out to California recently, she described her trip down the Baja Peninsula. Here is an excerpt:

> Palisades of ageless rock above a sweeping sea. Tall car-don cacti raising branched arms high, guardians of sand and scrub and thorn forests. Jagged mountains against sunset skies supersaturated with pinks, lemon yellows and hot orange . . .
>
> *(Reader's Digest,* July 1979)

High school students are also getting into the act. A number of English textbooks are presenting challenges such as asking them to write several pages on a penny or a pencil or a pebble, using all of the five senses. Desperate souls may right now be finishing the required assignment by gingerly using their sense of taste.

Now that you've made a pact with yourself to become more aware of what's going on in the world, you're ready to continue your search for ideas. Frankly, they are all around you. At first, they will appear to be nebulous, shapeless, and shadowy. But before you know it, they will take form and make you eager to communicate your findings. And then a surprising thing will happen—other ideas will pop up as you begin to pound your typewriter.

The Newspaper as Idea Source

Have you read your newspaper today? How about reading it again, but this time, with a cool, calculating eye toward article and story ideas. Several years ago, I spotted an item in a weekly paper that seemed to leap off the page and entice me into finding out some details.

I took it in to my writing class the next morning and all my students agreed with my reaction. The story revolved around an incident that took place in nearby Centreville, Virginia, in April of 1755 during the French and Indian War. According to an old legend, Major General Edward Braddock, a British general, was leading a division of Virginia riflemen and six companies of his regiment from Alexandria to Winchester. They were suddenly deluged by heavy rains and became bogged down by mud and branches of trees. The general decided that the only way to lighten the load was to abandon the $25,000 worth of gold coins he had brought for the payroll. He ordered several soldiers to dismount two cannons, fill them with the money, and then bury them in the mud. They were able to forge ahead, but Braddock was eventually killed and his papers were sent to England. Years later, an archivist found his report about the gold. Since that time, many people have visited Centreville to look for the buried treasure. It has never been found.

You can almost guess the rest of this story. Yes, we did venture out to find the two cannons and the gold. After doing a bit of research, we sallied forth one May morning armed with a metal detector, a camera, a map, and a picnic lunch. No, we didn't find the coins, but we did discover a painless way to have a lesson in American history. For a brief moment, we had made a dry subject come alive. And Dody Smith, one of my students, had the satisfaction of seeing her article on our expedition published in the *Arlington News*.

But you may be thinking that this type of story appears only once in a while. I can assure you that if you read your newspapers more carefully, you'll discover numerous nuggets of information that can be developed into salable material. I decided the other day to go through six newspapers I had on hand and look for items leading to some ideas for future articles. These are the ones that appealed to me:

1. People are living longer these days. More and more are reaching the one hundred mark. (What is their secret of longevity?)

2.   Hotline volunteers were honored at a luncheon yesterday and given awards. (How are they trained? What are some of the stories they hear? What advice do they give?)

3.   An art instructor says she has no qualms about teaching painting to prisoners at the county jail. (What other classes are taught in prison? Are inmates receiving recognition for their work?)

4.   For two years now, the residents in a small community have been hearing a high-pitched, keening sound in the middle of the night. (What other "monsters" have been reported throughout the country? Is there more truth than fiction to all of the stories?)

5.   This special test will reveal your psychic powers. (What are some of the new breakthroughs in parapsychology? Why are there more and more believers of psychic phenomena?)

6.   The right age to begin thinking about retirement is forty-five. (Why should it be done so early? What factors must be considered? Which one should be at the top of the list?)

These six items generated article ideas, but some of them can also be springboards for short story plots. What if . . . your protagonist is a young woman who becomes a hotline worker and manages to talk a young man out of taking an overdose of drugs by saying all the right things? And in doing so, she also saves herself: she, too, has suicidal tendencies. What if . . . your protagonist, the art teacher, falls in love with one of the prisoners? What if . . . your protagonist, a young man with ESP powers, falls in love with a beautiful young woman and realizes she is from another world?

But your newspaper has more to offer. Look for the ads called **Personals** which appear in daily publications, placed by people who want to give a message to an individual or a group. Behind each personal is a human-interest story. As you read the following four ads I borrowed from an English teacher's notebook, see what thoughts pop up in your mind and give you instant plots:

STEVE—Please call PAULA. Important! 555-8485

WEDDING GOWN, VEIL, size 14, bridesmaids' dresses, 2 ring pillows. New—never worn. 321-7592

MISS JOHNSON—I have a job for you. Call 632-6788

WANTED—Man with spirit and empty barn. Please contact the Honorable J. Shortell, mayor of Georgetown 1966-69. 339-4677

These were actual ads, culled from several papers. If you are especially interested in fiction, get into the habit of turning to the page where the personals are listed. You'll find some that are poignant; a few that are humorous; and a number that are downright intriguing. Here is your chance to let your imagination take free rein. Let it run wild; immediately jot down your ideas for characters and plots and settings.

You can see from these examples that the newspaper is a valuable source of inspiration for writers of fiction or nonfiction.

Magazines

Magazines, of course, also lend themselves to article ideas and story lines. Plan now to spend an hour or two in the library whenever you can browsing through the magazine section. If you haven't done that for a while, you're in for a surprise. You'll find many new publications covering all kinds of subjects, including hobbies, astronomy, history, and health. Thumb through them and you'll probably come across some of the following items:

- That "junk" in your attic may be more valuable than you think.
- The moon can be held responsible for some of your moods.
- Some scientists believe that black holes could be the key to the secrets of the universe.
- The Mormons have a lower cancer rate and have fewer heart attacks than the rest of us.
- It's possible that there really was a King Arthur and that he is now resting with his fair queen in Glastonbury Abbey in England.
- Feeling depressed? The experts say you can think your way out of those low periods.
- The "Share-a-Home" concept is gaining momentum with senior citizens throughout the country.

- With a little bit of know-how, you can interpret your own dreams.
- Simple changes in your lifestyle can prolong your life.
- What you can do if diets don't work for you.
- American adults are going back to school and taking courses that range from flower arranging to auto mechanics.
- The Voyager 1 space probe revealed a world so strange that it defied known laws of astronomy.
- There is a way to prepare for the "empty nest" syndrome.
- What is the laser doing in the field of medicine?
- Is it true that teachers can't teach?
- How you can prevent an affair.
- How you can survive an audit by the IRS.

What variations on these themes can you come up with?

As you look through the magazines, pay attention to the number of **how-to's.** If you have a flair for this kind of writing, you're bound to find a market for a well-written, explicitly detailed piece. Those that appear almost every month are: how to shop and save; how to make a diet work; how to grow African violets; how to keep from growing old; how to beat inflation; how to run a yard sale. Even though these features are done again and again, you can add your special touch to them and make them unique. If you have found that your shopping bill is less when you leave your spouse at home, weave that fact into your article. If you used a buddy system on your last diet, tell about it in your article; describe how it helped you and your best friend lose those pounds. If you began to jog at the age of fifty or sixty and became healthier in mind and body, share your secret with the rest of us. If you turned your yard sale into a block affair and made some extra dollars, give us the details.

Books

Books can also be a fount of ideas for articles and fillers. If you are interested in writing inspirational material, for example, re-read *The Power of Positive Thinking* by Norman Vincent Peale.

Why was his book so successful? Why is it still read today? What are your suggestions for positive thinking? If you read *The Cosmic Connection* by Carl Sagan, you'll not only have an update on our nine planets, but a description of Venus that fits our conception of hell. Dr. Sagan says that this planet is "sizzling, choking, sulfurous, and red." Do you believe there is a hell? Where is it? Is it a place or a state of mind? During the past ten years, this subject hasn't been discussed too often in the churches. With the renewed interest in religion, this may be the time to do a feature on this topic for a magazine.

Biographies of famous men and women have much to offer the beginning writer. A few years ago, I began to read profiles of the writers I admired and of a few other heroes. I was amazed at the wealth of information I acquired in just a few months. As my notebook became crammed with facts, I wondered what I could do with them. A short time later, I spied a notice on the bulletin board at the high school where I was substituting. A publisher in Michigan was looking for stories about famous people or events to use for his educational publications in elementary grades. I sent him vignettes on the lives of Mary Shelley, Nathan Hale, Robert Louis Stevenson, Jules Verne, and Christopher Columbus. He liked the way I started each story—strong leads that caught the attention of the young reader. He also approved of the intriguing facts I used: Mary Shelley wrote her tale of horror from a nightmare she had on a stormy night; Nathan Hale was probably turned in by his cousin; Robert Louis Stevenson gave away his birthday to a little girl; Jules Verne was a hundred years ahead of his time and "went" to the moon in 1865; Columbus was tall, redheaded, and freckled.

Are you in the middle of another book besides this one? If you are, don't be surprised if an idea for an article or story suddenly storms into your consciousness and won't leave. Jot it down at once. When Midge Papich, one of my students, read *Nicholas and Alexandra*, she was so impressed with the Easter gifts the tsars of Russia gave their wives that she decided to write about them. These were the famous jewel-encrusted eggs made by Fabergé between 1885 and 1917. Each one of them contained a surprise, ranging from a gold miniature of the palace to a ruby pendant. Midge did her research, and on Easter morning of that year her article appeared in the *Washington Post*. When Muriel McKenna came across a reference to the history of gloves in a book that she was reading, she wanted to know more. She, too, did some research, wrote a feature, and had it published in a weekly paper.

Have you seen a copy of *The People's Almanac* (Doubleday, 1975)? Now here's a delightful way to search for ideas. It was compiled by Irving Wallace and his son David Wallechinsky, and claims to be "the first reference book ever prepared to be read for pleasure." It's equal in size to ten books, and you won't be able to tuck it under your arm or into your purse. But you'll want to. Some of its facts you'll want to research are:

- Photographs taken by Skylab may have located the remains of Noah's Ark.
- Adolf Hitler owned 8,960 acres of land in Colorado.
- There is more than $4 billion in lost or buried treasure scattered throughout the United States.
- Guards at the Alamos, Mexico, jail have to serve out the sentences of any prisoners who escape while they are on duty.
- Harvey Kennedy invented the shoelace and made $2.5 million on his patent.

The book, of course, contains many detailed articles on every subject imaginable. You will be interested to know that freelancers contributed many of the stories and were listed in the credits in the front of the book. Dody Smith, who wrote about our search for Braddock's gold, was assigned to do a follow-up on what happened to the *Bounty* mutineers. And there on page 516 is her fascinating account of what she discovered about Pitcairn Island.

Other Idea Sources

Other ideas for writing can stem from being a good listener. From now on, pay more attention to what your friends and relatives are saying. Not too long ago, a friend of mine told me about the beer bread she was planning to make for her chili supper that night. We were standing in line at the supermarket, and before long she had quite an audience. She said that she had gotten the recipe from an all-night disc jockey who mentioned it casually to fill some airtime. All you need is three cups of self-rising flour, three tablespoons sugar, and one can (twelve ounces) of beer. Mix the ingredients lightly. Pour at once into a well-greased pan. Bake in a 375° oven for forty-five minutes. Voila! You not only have a unique loaf of bread but a great conversation piece at the table. I wasn't surprised when it appeared in print the following week. Someone had been shrewd enough to realize that this recipe would find a ready market—and was right on target.

If you become a good listener, you may even hear some unusual **stories and legends.** Stashed away in the ragbag of my mind is a tale told in Europe that the devil takes human form once a year for twenty-four hours and can appear anywhere he wishes. Only last week at a writers' meeting, an Irishman said that in his country there is a legend that God takes human form once a year for a day and night and visits a different country each time. What if . . . they both took the same day and met? What if . . . a young woman was seated in a restaurant or inn across from a handsome stranger and found herself almost mesmerized by his eyes? Who would he be? Satan or God?

Ideas can also come from your **family life.** Have you gone through a divorce and survived? Are you a new stepparent? Have you gone back to work after twenty years? Are you going back to school to get that degree? Have you volunteered to be a surrogate mother? Has your son or daughter succumbed to drugs? Are you dreading the whole idea of retirement? Is your family life happy? If it is, do share your secret with those people who believe that the family unit will soon be a thing of the past.

Holidays can also furnish some subjects to write about. Check the newspapers and magazines and save the items that tell about the origins of Halloween or Thanksgiving or Yom Kippur or Christmas. But when you do your own research, include those tidbits that add a special touch to your filler or article. Did you know that Christmas once was banned in Boston? Did you know that the first Thanksgiving lasted for three days?

Do you have a **hobby?** Write about it. The men and women in my writing classes during the past fourteen years have turned their expertise in cooking, magic, book-collecting, gardening, poetry writing, travel, and Virginia history into bylines and some pocket money. Wade Fleetwood's hobby of collecting grains of sand from all over the world is always a conversation maker. Not only has he written it up, but he himself has been interviewed and featured in several publications. He keeps the grains of sand in glass vials; the reporters are fascinated by the colors, which range from a blush pink to a charcoal gray.

Can you remember your **dreams?** Good! You already have a source for ideas for your writing. But since they can vanish so quickly, stumble over to your notebook when you awaken and scribble some key words which will help you reconstruct what happened. It is said that Robert Louis Stevenson could dream plots at will. His famous story *Dr. Jekyll and Mr. Hyde* came to him one night almost in its entirety and he sat down the next morning and wrote it all down. Samuel Coleridge's poem "Kubla Khan" also came from a dream. But there is a footnote to this story. As he was sitting at his desk scribbling away, someone knocked on the door. When he returned, he couldn't remember how his dream ended. If you read the poem, you will see that it is unfinished. If you have a nightmare now and then, hang on to it. As noted earlier, Mary Shelley wrote *Frankenstein* after she experienced a terrifying vision on a stormy night.

Now that you have finished reading this chapter, it is time for you to begin writing. Choose one of the subjects listed on these pages. Add to it from your memories or expertise. Round it out by information from your local library. Nurture it day after day in your thoughts. The time will come when you will want to get it all down on paper and share it with the world.

But you can reach that point only if you start now!

3

Tools of the Trade

Whether you write fiction or nonfiction, you will need certain tools to help you become a selling writer. Heading the list is a good dictionary. There are many good ones available, but many publishing houses and magazines seem to prefer *Webster's Eighth New Collegiate Dictionary*, which contains biographies and geographical names at the back. You should also take a look at *The American Heritage Dictionary of the English Language* and *Funk and Wagnall's Standard College Dictionary*. All three of these books, which are abridged (that is, they have fewer words and shorter definitions), come highly recommended. If, later on, you want to invest in a large, unabridged version, browse through *Webster's Third New International Dictionary* or *The Random House Dictionary of the English Language*.

Another reference book you should keep within arm's reach of your typewriter is a copy of *Roget's Thesaurus of Words and Phrases*. When the exact word to describe something eludes you, this book of synonyms will save you time and frustration. You'll also improve your vocabulary. Look for the one that is arranged alphabetically; it's much easier to use than the original version. It comes in hardcover and in an abridged pocket edition. Webster also puts out a book of synonyms with detailed explanations of the distinctions among words of similar meanings. Both books will come to the rescue of the writer in search of a word.

How's your spelling? If this subject gave you trouble in school and is still the bane of your existence, take heart. You can now find a pocketbook speller at many bookstores; it contains only words, no definitions. It should prove a boon to all of you future writers who are never sure how a word is spelled.

If you don't have a set of encyclopedias at home, this is the time to scout around and buy one on sale. I've never regretted buying the World Book series fifteen years ago, when I was more of a teacher than a writer. Since then, I have received fifteen annuals that updated many of the subjects described in the books. I especially like the format because I can find things quickly, and it is easy to understand. You may want to take a look at the *Encyclopae-*

dia Britannica and the Encyclopedia Americana; both are excellent and will give you the facts you need. You'll find them a little more scholarly than the World Book series.

It's important to own an encyclopedia because it will save you time. Whenever an idea for a story or article suddenly descends upon you, your A-to-Z books are right there to give information. You won't have to dash to the library until it's necessary to round out your material with books written on the subject. You'll be amazed how often you'll use this reference tool as you become a professional writer.

Armed with these basics, you should be able to turn out a credible manuscript. But the more you write, the more critical you'll become of what you are producing. You'll worry about the mechanics of writing, and wonder if your commas are all in the right place. The best two dollars you'll ever spend is for a slim paperback called The Elements of Style by William Strunk, Jr., and E.B. White. It was originally written by Professor Strunk when he taught English at Cornell University more than sixty years ago. E.B. White was a student there and found himself greatly impressed with the professor and his course. In 1957, he was commissioned by the Macmillan Publishing Company to make some revisions. (In addition to being a master stylist himself, he is also a humorist and essayist, longtime contributor to The New Yorker, and the author of Charlotte's Web and Stuart Little, two popular children's books.) He was delighted to do so and added a chapter of his own. It lends a special touch to Will Strunk's rules of rhetoric.

This little book will teach you many things. Some of them are:

- Write in a way that comes naturally.
- Work from a suitable design.
- Write with nouns and verbs.
- Avoid the use of qualifiers.
- Omit needless words.

E.B. White emphasizes the fact that William Strunk told his students over and over that every good writer must omit unnecessary words. This rule is one of the most difficult to follow. Many beginning writers—and some professionals—find it painful to go through a manuscript and cut out words and phrases that took time and effort to produce. But you can do it. Keep telling yourself that even the best writers find it agonizing to streamline their work. Eventually, you'll make every word count.

The best training I've ever had along these lines was years ago when I wrote 365 radio scripts for a syndicate in Kansas City, Missouri. Each script was only sixty seconds long and had to tell something about every day of the year. My producer showed me how to take details about a holiday or an event or a famous person and make them become a dramatic minute. There were times when I thought it just couldn't be done and wished I had never signed the contract for the job. But the challenge forced me to choose every word carefully and in such a way that the listener was impressed with what he heard. My best one-minute script read:

(June 18)

The cold, penetrating rain slashed against the general's face, and he shivered as he turned up the collar of his great-coat. It had been raining for hours, and when dawn came, he decided not to drag his artillery across the soggy fields. It was a decision which would be recorded in history forever. Napoleon Bonaparte, one of the greatest military geniuses of all time, who "aimed his army like a pistol," waited for a sun which never appeared. At 11:30 on the morning of June 18, he ordered his French troops to attack the Duke of Wellington's army in the Belgian town of Waterloo. But while the general tarried with his men, Marshal von Blucher and his weary Prussian soldiers had slogged through the mud to reinforce the British military units. Napoleon's defeat was so overwhelming that when someone now suffers a disastrous setback, we say he has "met his Waterloo."

From now on, use vivid verbs and concrete nouns instead of all those adjectives and adverbs. Professor Strunk said it first; it's become a cardinal rule in my class and one that I repeat often. If you need some coaching in vivid verbs, read the sports page in your daily newspaper. There you'll find such things as:

Maryland Rips Vanderbilt
Middies Stun Washington

Royals Rout Yanks
SMU Rocks Texas
Astros Whip Phillies
Chinaglia Ignites Cosmos

If you're a poetry buff, you'll also find some vivid verbs in your favorite poems. These four lines from one of John Donne's religious sonnets are a good example:

Batter my heart, three-personed God; for you
As yet but knock, breathe, shine, and seek to mend
That I may rise and stand, o'erthrow me and bend
Your force to break, blow, burn and make me new.

From now on, train yourself to use action verbs. Don't always have your character *walk* into a room; have him *shuffle, stagger, saunter, swagger,* or *slink* in. But one word of caution: don't go overboard on this kind of writing. Reading the sports page and poetry should only be a training exercise. And what about that verb *said?* There's no reason why you can't use *grumbled* or *called* or *shouted,* but do it in moderation.

And what about the use of concrete nouns? This may be a little more difficult to do, but once you get into the habit of doing it, your troubles are over. It should be pointed out that concrete nouns are useful in description because the reader can picture them in his mind. For example, if you simply say that your grandson raises flowers for a hobby, it doesn't mean much. But if you tell us that he raises lavender orchids, we immediately can see them. Whenever you can, turn that house into a cabin; that tree into an elm; that boat into a tramp steamer; and that cat into a gray-striped tabby.

Don't abandon all of your adverbs and adjectives. But do choose them very carefully. Make every one count. The right adjective can be another tool in your writing kit. If you're describing an apple, it's much more effective if you tell us that it is wormy instead of red. If your writing seems to abound with too many qualifiers, cut out *very* and *pretty* and *big* and *little.* But if they are necessary once in a while, use more colorful synonyms. Something *big* can be *grand* or *gigantic* or *massive.* Something *little* can be *diminutive* or *wee* or *tiny.*

Improving your vocabulary is another way in which you can

make your writing more dynamic and alive. There are supposed to be about 600,000 words in the English language, but even the most learned people seldom use more than 24,000 different words during the course of their lives. The more words you acquire, the easier it will be to find the right ones to express your thoughts. One of the best ways to increase your vocabulary is to read, read, read. Whenever a strange word pops up, reach for the dictionary and learn its meaning.

If you were asked to give the ten most beautiful words in the English language, what would your answer be? According to *The New Webster Encyclopedic Dictionary*, they are:

lullaby	soul
murmuring	golden
noble	glow
slumber	twilight
melody	home

You must admit that these words are pleasant to the ear, but why don't you work on a list of your own? Thumb through some of your favorite passages in your favorite books, and jot down those nouns and adjectives which appeal to you. Watch for others as you read current magazines or novels; add them to your list. You may even want to collect words you find ugly or jarring. Become a wordsmith, an expert on words, and when you do, be ready for an exhilarating and exciting experience. Nathaniel Hawthorne said, "Words—so innocent and powerless as they are, as standing in a dictionary, how potent for good and evil they become, in the hands of one who knows how to combine them." Here is your chance to learn how to choose the right combination and communicate your ideas to the world.

Additional Helps

The basic tools I've discussed will give you the necessary assists in becoming a professional writer; here are some "nice to have" reference works you can pick up as your checks come in:

• *The Careful Writer* by Theodore M. Bernstein is a delightful book which will tell you such things as when to use *farther* and *further* and how to avoid split infinitives. Mr. Bernstein writes in a witty style that is easy to understand.

• The *Columbia-Viking Desk Encyclopedia* is a one-volume book with condensed information on an amazing number of subjects. It's the best of its kind and is a great time-saver. The paperback edition is also a money-saver.

• The *Reader's Encyclopedia* by William Rose Benet is a book that will hold you entranced with its information about authors, places, characters, literary works, and even words. I can't remember when I latched on to it, but every time I bring my two copies into my classroom, my students spirit them away to devour some of their fascinating facts. Since I began to immerse myself in its pages, I have learned that it's quite possible that the Fountain of Youth is on Bimini Island in the Bahamas; the Holy Grail came into the possession of Joseph of Arimathea and then eventually passed down to Sir Galahad, his last descendant; it's possible that Pontius Pilate became a Christian and repented of his sins; and that Cervantes was captured by Barbary pirates and held as a slave in Algiers for five years. The subjects are arranged in dictionary form. Turn to any page and you'll pick up an idea for research or for writing a story.

• *Bartlett's Familiar Quotations* will wend its way into your writing more than you think. There will be times when you are scurrying around for a phrase that will add a special touch or accent to your article, or you have to track down who said this or that on a certain subject. It is arranged chronologically by authors quoted and has a key-word index. There are several others on the market, but this is the best.

• The *World Almanac* will supply you with information on events of the previous year, statistics on populations, profiles on famous people, facts about countries, and more. You may want to buy *The New York Times Encyclopedic Almanac:* it contains such things as a calendar of events of a hundred years ago and even a list of endangered wildlife.

Many of these reference books, of course, can be found at your library. But in addition to the encyclopedias, dictionaries, and almanacs, you'll find a wealth of material waiting for you the minute you walk in the door. This is the time for you to become acquainted with your reference librarian so that he can point out the following:

- *The Readers' Guide to Periodical Literature* is an index of articles in more than 160 magazines published in the United States. It is an excellent source of current information and will save you all kinds of time. As soon as you have an idea for an article, check this guide to see what has already been written on the subject. Author and subject entries are combined in one alphabetical index, and each one gives the necessary details for finding the articles in the magazines. A list of abbreviations used in the guide appears in the front of every issue. *The Readers' Guide* is published twice a month, with cumulative issues appearing at the end of every year.

- *Who's Who in America, Who's Who in the World,* and *Who Was Who in America* will help you find information on men and women of today and yesterday. And you'll enjoy looking up facts in *Current Biography,* which will reveal that Julia Child, the TV cook, wanted to be a spy during World War II and that Jean-Claude Killy started skiing when he was only three years old.

- Joseph Kane's *Famous First Facts* will fill you in on all kinds of unusual information, including tidbits on the first balloon, the first ice cream sundae, and the first library. His *Facts about the Presidents* will give you details on the men in the White House, but it will also draw comparisons among our leaders along the lines of religion, their age when they took office, etc.

- Frank Magill's *Masterplots* will give you plot summaries of more than two thousand novels, plays, and essays. His *Masterpieces of World Philosophy* in summary form will supply you with facts about the major philosophies and religions, ranging from Plato to Sartre.

While you are at the library, become acquainted with the shelves that contain the books on creative writing. Here you'll find material on how to write fillers, articles, columns, short stories, novels, nonfiction books, and children's stories. Now is the time to pick up a copy of *The Writer* and *Writer's Digest,* two magazines that provide advice and up-to-date markets. They will also suggest a number of books the library doesn't have on hand so that you can build your own reference material around the category in which you are interested.

Before you leave the library, ask one of the librarians to show you where the *vertical file* is located. It is often overlooked and yet it may have just what you have been looking for. It usually contains information on current topics; pamphlets published by government agencies, museums, and industries; newspaper clippings; photographs of important events; local history, etc. These items are filed standing on edge and are often found in a big drawer in the main room.

If your library is a large one, you can become acquainted with *The New York Times Index;* it will prove invaluable in your research projects. This index is bound in annual volumes and is arranged chronologically under subject headings with date, page, and column references. By checking with this index, you will get the gist of what the *Times* printed about your subject; later, you can go to the back files either in bound form or on microfilm to read the articles themselves. If your library does not have this index, call one of your nearby universities.

Two books that you'll find helpful in any kind of research that you do are *Finding Facts Fast* by Alden Todd and *Who-What-When-Where-How-Why* by Mona McCormack. The first one is based on methods used by librarians, scholars, investigative reporters, and detectives. "The shortest path between two facts may well be Alden Todd," said Alvin Toffler, author of *Future Shock* and *The Third Wave*, who was impressed by Todd's shortcuts to information. The second book was written by a woman who worked in the editorial reference library at the *New York Times*. Her book does much to take the "search" out of research and tells students and writers where to look up what. It starts out by describing the various types of reference books and how to decide, for example, whether you need a multivolume encyclopedia or a paperback almanac.

4

Try a Filler First

Now that you are inspired to put words to paper, what should you write? How should you begin to communicate your thoughts and ideas and observations to the world? "Great oaks from little acorns grow" is a trite but true statement; it really is a good idea to start out with short items or fillers.

What is a filler exactly? There was a time when it meant an item used to fill the end of a column at the bottom of a page in a newspaper or magazine. Though this is still true to a certain extent today, the filler has come into its own. Editors realize that their readers look for those little items that intrigue them or make them chuckle. Some writers send out two or three or more fillers a week to make pocket money. You can concentrate on this field alone and make enough to pay for a mini-vacation twice a year.

A filler can range from a phrase to a personal experience running about 500 words. It can be a pun, a quip, an epigram, a household hint, a food fact, a footnote to history, light verse, a recipe, a joke, a puzzle, a how-to hint, a daffy definition, a child's bright saying, an anecdote, or a typographical error. On the following pages, you'll find some examples of these fillers, and don't be surprised if they jog your memory. Be sure to jot down ideas for these whenever they occur. Don't depend on your memory for remembering tidbits of information; they are elusive, and some never come back.

If you have a flair for **plays on words,** capitalize on it; you will find a ready market out there. *Reader's Digest* is one of the popular markets for this kind of filler. Here are two I think are excellent (they were sent in by freelancers):

Clock-eyed students waiting for the big hand to reach summer.

(Gloria Schlesna, *Reader's Digest*, June 1969)

Joggers: Sole brothers.

(M. Randisi, *Reader's Digest*, June 1969)

Would you like to try a **quip?** This is a clever or witty remark such as:

> People are like plants—some go to seed with age, others go to pot.

> Plenty of people have a good aim in life, but a lot of them don't know when to pull the trigger.

> Pollution costs us millions; grime doesn't pay.
> (*Senior Scribes*, June 1981)

(*Senior Scribes* began a year ago when I had lunch with two of my writers. One of them, Pauline Reiher, was trying to get into a new category of writing; I suggested that she try a newsletter. She thought it was a wonderful idea and went to work immediately. There are now 180 subscribers, mainly in the Arlington area, but some copies are sent to other states where friends and relatives live. This monthly newsletter is actually a magazine. It contains recipes, household hints, medical tips, poems, nostalgia, jokes, footnotes to history, quips, travel notes, etc. In other words, it's a true filler market.)

An **epigram,** according to the dictionary, is "any witty, ingenious, or pointed saying tersely expressed." It is a slice of life reaching a wide group of readers. Without a doubt, Ben Franklin found this kind of writing easy to do, and his *Poor Richard's Almanac* is full of pointed sayings:

> God helps them that help themselves.

> Those have a short Lent who owe Money to be paid at Easter.

An up-to-date epigram comes from the pen of humorist Sam Levenson, who wrote:

> A sweater is a garment that a child wears because his mother is cold.

If you have a penchant for **light verse,** cultivate it! Editors are always looking for this kind of material. Richard Armour is a master at this form of writing and these four lines made him famous:

Going to Extremes

Shake and shake
the catsup bottle.
None will come,
And then a lot'll.

(*Light Armour*, McGraw-Hill, 1954)

Household hints can usually find a ready market and they are
fun to write. Begin now to draw upon your own experiences, and to
thumb through magazines and newspapers for ideas. Check with
members of your family; they may have old almanacs around or a
family recipe that dates back many years. Nostalgia is "in." Put
your memory to work and capitalize on it. What was it that made
your Thanksgiving dinner extra-special? What did your Aunt Jen-
nie do to make her children's parties so successful? What was your
Uncle Joe's remedy for soothing poison ivy? What did your mother
concoct for the racking cough you had after a cold?

If you are thinking that these bits of information are trivial,
think again. Begin to collect them now. They may lead to something big. A case in point: two enterprising women named Mary
Ellen Pinkham and Pearl Higginbotham recently turned out a book
of ways to solve common household problems and saw it top the
paperback bestseller list. They probably never dreamed that their
collection of little how-to's would do such a thing. Here are a few
of their tips that are different and very helpful:

- Store cottage cheese upside down. It will keep longer.
- To keep lettuce fresh, store it in the refrigerator in paper
bags instead of cellophane.
- To clean eyeglasses without streaks, use a drop of vinegar
or vodka on each lens.
- When postage stamps are stuck together, place them in the
freezer.
- For your plants, use water at room temperature. Let water
stand for a day to get rid of chlorine. Better yet, use old fizzless
club soda—it has just the right chemicals to add vigor to your
plants.

• If there's a bee—or any winged insect—in the house, reach for the hair spray. This stiffens their wings and immobilizes them immediately.
(*Mary Ellen's Best of Helpful Hints*, Warner Books, 1979)

This is a category that intrigues me; I have been collecting similar items for years. Mine aren't as clever as Mary Ellen's, but some of mine may motivate you to write down some of yours and get you started in this category:

• You forgot to take the frozen ground meat out of the freezer before you went off for the day? Shred the meat on a rough cabbage shredder by holding the whole frozen block in one hand as if it were a head of cabbage.
• An apple corer is a good tool to use when transplanting tiny seedlings; it does less damage than a trowel would and makes handling the delicate plants much easier.
• Raw eggs spilled on the kitchen floor make a gooey mess, but if you cover them with salt for twenty minutes you'll have no trouble sweeping them up.
• A few cloves in the corners of your shelves and cupboards will discourage ants and give a spicy smell to your cabinets.
• If a piece of Great-Aunt Margaret's tea set is cracked but not broken, boil it in milk for forty-five minutes. The crack will disappear and the china strengthen.
• Meat can be reheated to its original goodness for a late guest if it is placed in a heavy skillet, covered with lettuce leaves and a lid, and then heated in a moderate oven for a short time.

Now that there is a renewed interest in the culinary arts, **food facts** will always find a ready market. But before you go hunting down some of them, try a **recipe** first. Do your buffet suppers always have the guests coming back for more? Do they always ask for the recipe? Is it fairly inexpensive? Write it up and send it off to a market. You will find food facts when you least expect them. I came across this tidbit in a daily newspaper a few years ago:

The largest single dish in the world is roasted camel, prepared occasionally for Bedouin wedding feasts. Cooked eggs are stuffed into fish, the fish stuffed into cooked chickens, the chickens stuffed into a roasted sheep carcass and the sheep stuffed into a whole camel.

Are you a **history** buff? You may want to collect items that revolve around historical figures or events. If you have always been a great admirer of Robert E. Lee, write up the fact that at the beginning of the Civil War, he was asked to lead the Union troops. If you have always been intrigued with Cleopatra, do a filler that describes her as a fascinating conversationalist, a first-rate military strategist, and a remarkable actress instead of a wanton seductress. If you have some expertise on the Revolutionary War, write an anecdote about Samuel Adams's dog, who bit only Redcoats.

Footnotes to history make interesting reading. During the Bicentennial, I wrote over two hundred radio scripts in which I pretended to be a journalist who lived two centuries ago. Later, I wrote fillers and articles, telling my readers that dinner at Mount Vernon began promptly at 3 p.m.; George Washington's favorite wine was Madeira; dessert was usually strawberry tarts or whiskey pie; the general had only one ambition: to become the country's leading agriculturalist; two hundred years ago, backgammon was popular; only seven planets were known to be in existence; and the mint julep and the cocktail came into being.

Speaking of backgammon, how's your game? Do you know anything about its origin? Do some research and you'll be amazed at what you'll find. Its history can be traced back five thousand years. It was fashionable in ancient Greece and Rome; Plato mentions it, and the Emperor Caligula reportedly cheated at it. Cleopatra, by the way, was a whiz at the game. If you like **games and cards,** find out something about them and your filler material will almost write itself.

How are you at **puzzles?** If you can compose a crossword from scratch, you'll have no trouble finding a market. But since they are difficult to do, you may want to try your hand at this kind of filler:

On Dec. 17, 1903, Orville Wright made a brief but historical trip by plane. Each of the following fictional characters below also made a famous trip—but by what means of transportation?

1. Casey Jones	1. Train
2. Cinderella	2. Coach
3. Hans Brinker	3. Ice skates
4. The Joad Family	4. Truck
5. Huckleberry Finn	5. Raft
6. Phileas Fogg	6. Balloon
7. Eliza	7. Ice floes
8. Winken, Blinken, and Nod	8. Wooden shoe

(*Modern Maturity*, Dec.-Jan., 1971)

Are you getting ready to **travel?** Taking a trip to England? Make sure to stop off at the British Museum in London and look for the mummy of an Egyptian woman said to be five thousand years old. Her fingernails, painted dark red, will give you an intriguing little filler. You'll also pick up some filler material if you sign up for the tour that takes you to haunted castles. Before you go, see what you can find out about King Harold or Lawrence of Arabia. The ghosts of both of them go wandering about, according to townsfolk.

Are you the joker in your crowd? Capitalize on your talent and write down the **jokes** you do so well. One word of caution: Study the magazines and observe the way their jokes are written up. Notice how they begin, how they begin to build, and how everything depends on the right kind of punch line.

Is **astronomy** your hobby? Share some of your findings with your earthling friends and tell them about the awesome universe. More and more people are becoming interested in the heavens and outer space. Tell them that we all came from the stars a long time ago and reveal to them that there are at least a hundred billion other galaxies whirling through space—there must be different kinds of life out there whether we want to believe it or not. And what are black holes? Can you explain them in layman's language? All of these items can be written up as fillers or articles.

Have you always had an interest in the signs of the zodiac? What do you really know about it? Have you read Linda Goodman's book on **astrology?** She'll tell you so many intimate details about your life that you'll believe she's your alter ego. Here's your chance to do some fascinating research. You'll discover that it all began more than five thousand years ago in the

Persian Gulf area—and you'll come across many intriguing facts that will lend themselves to filler material (and articles). Do you know why there are twelve people on a jury? The story is told that many years ago, a defendant was sure that the only way he could get a fair trial was to have all the signs of the zodiac represented. In your own research, find out what famous people in history had their own astrologers. Who are the VIPs of today who don't make a move without their signs being read? Why is this pseudo-science so popular today?

It's just possible that you are a collector of **strange and unusual facts.** If they are not too far out and make good reading, keep on collecting them. You should be able to find a market if they sound something like the following:

- It takes seventeen muscles to smile and forty-three to frown.

- The average heart beats 100,000 times every day.

- Taking a bite of another's hamburger is against the law in Oklahoma.

- In New Jersey, you can be arrested for slurping your soup in a restaurant.

If **Christmas** is one of your favorite holidays, you should be able to find a market for your items every year. Do you know some folklore about animals or the weather or decorations? There is much of it relating to December 25, and people like to read about it again and again. Do some browsing at the library and find out what happened to the Three Wise Men after they left Bethlehem. Find out why Christmas was banned in Boston during the colonial period.

Be sure to write your fillers and mail them to the magazine at least six months ahead of time. (All seasonal material should be done this way.) You'll find it strange to think about Christmas on a sunny day in June! But before long, it will seem the natural thing to do.

Are you superstitious? Then you'll enjoy collecting material aimed for Halloween or Friday the Thirteenth. But don't be content with the ordinary ones: walking under ladders; avoiding black cats; spilling salt at the table, etc. Try to find some **family superstitions** that will make interesting reading today. When my students reminisced, they came up with unusual ones: if you go out one door, come back in through another; if you are stirring batter, stir in only one direction; don't ever have two clocks ticking in the same room; make sure you never put a hat on your bed. You may want to do some research on Friday the 13th; no one seems to know why it is associated with bad luck. You'll be surprised by the details you'll find if you do some research at the library.

And while you're checking with your family about superstitions, see if they can remember any **quotes** and profound sayings of Uncle George or Grandpa Miller. Look up some of the philosophical lines that have always appealed to you through the years. Write them down in your notebook. *Reader's Digest* may be just the market for your material. If you can find a longer quote from a book you've read recently, a passage you especially liked, send it off to *Book Digest*. (You'll find the address in Chapter 11.) You'll make a pretty penny and share your filler with many readers. It, too, must be witty or wise.

There is a new kind of filler making its appearance lately, and some of you may have a flair for this kind of writing. Do you find yourself enjoying the **bumper sticker sayings** as you drive along the highways? An old one that impressed me said "Wise men still seek Him." A new one that made me grin said "I finally got it all together—and now I don't know where I put it." Be on the lookout for other signs and then try doing some of your own. It's definitely a growing market.

You may even find an idea for a filler in the preface of a book. If you pick up a copy of Walter Lord's *A Night to Remember,* you'll discover a story within a story. In 1898, a struggling writer by the name of Morgan Robertson wrote a novel about a luxury liner full of rich people enjoying themselves. Robertson created a tragedy: the ship struck an iceberg and went down in the murky waters of the Atlantic on a cold April night. Many lives were lost on a steamer that was supposed to be unsinkable. Does all of this sound familiar? It should. On April 10, 1912, a real ship left Southhampton, England, on her maiden voyage to New York. She, too, struck an iceberg, and more than 1,400 lives were lost. She was called the *Titanic*; the imaginary one was named the *Titan*. It is ironic to note that Robertson's story didn't make much of an impression on the reading public. In fact, his tales of the sea only won the recognition they deserved years after he had died.

Do you have a pet peeve? Do you know someone who has done good in your community? Were you helped by a stranger when your car fell apart on the highway? Do you have a poignant story to tell about your old tiger cat or the mutt you recently acquired? Did your young son or granddaughter regale your guests with a funny remark or a shrewd observation? Do you have an anecdote to tell that is bizarre or humorous or startling? These subjects are also grist for the filler mill. Another source, of course, is your public library. Here you can go through some of the encyclopedias and other tomes—but be careful. Don't wind up with a filler that sounds stilted and dull. Accept the challenge to make it sound exciting and unusual; put your creative talents to work. While you are browsing about, check the magazines for filler markets. Become acquainted with new publications. Look for some of the magazines that seem to suit your style and material.

Getting Organized

Make sure to buy a small notebook for all your jottings. No writer can depend entirely on his memory; don't expect yours to be different. This tool of yours should be able to fit into a purse or pocket. It doesn't sound like much, but you won't be able to live without it from now on. Take it with you on the plane and train and bus. Use it in the doctor's office or the dentist's waiting room. If you decide to concentrate on filler writing, this kind of notebook is a must and will pay dividends in a few months.

As you scout around for ideas, be sure to come up with some kind of filing system. Some writers mark large brown envelopes with various categories, and whenever they come across any material pertaining to those subjects, they slide them in. But there is an easier way: use any empty shoe box, one with a cover. Your notes and clippings are much more accessible that way. (Whenever you see something you are sure you can use, you just toss it into the box instead of filing it away.) Later on, you can buy a small filing cabinet and organize your fillers in a more orderly fashion. But when you are starting out, keep your filing system as simple as possible.

If you're all set to send your fillers to *Reader's Digest,* a magazine known the world over for its readable nuggets of information, look before you leap and crawl before you walk. Most of my students take it for granted that it's a breeze to get published in this magazine. I always have to remind them that there is stiff competition. I also add that anecdotes and personal experience pieces are especially difficult to do. To convince them, I have them choose one from the magazine and write it down word for word. It doesn't take long for them to realize that there is a beginning, a middle, and an end, and that the words seem to flow. They usually agree to try the small markets first, and then aim for the big one. You can benefit from this advice even if you are set upon sending your materials to *Reader's Digest.* It will help make your filler more polished and give you a fighting chance to get accepted.

Manuscript Format

You are finally ready to mail out your little items—jokes and household hints and footnotes to history and personal experiences. Aside from the fact that they should be typed, what should they look like? What you are sending should look like this:

Henry M. Jones
236 Miller Lane   Appr. 120 words
Arlington, Va. 22205

HUMOR IN UNIFORM
Every year on April Fool's Day, my thoughts go back to
what happened to Sgt. Billings that morning.

But suppose there is no definite category for your item. Then what? Your best bet is to do it this way (you are mailing in a recipe story to the *Washington Post):*

Carol Jennings
5307 Kensington St.   Appr. 220 words
Silver Spring, Md. 33604

FOOD SECTION

One afternoon in 1830, Col. Robert Johnson stood on the steps of the courthouse in Salem, New Jersey, and performed a daring deed: he ate a tomato. Spectators were horrified and predicted he would be dead by morning.

Of course nothing happened, although through the centuries the idea has persisted that the succulent tomato. . .

Mailing and Marketing

A filler can be folded and placed in a long (No. 10) white envelope. Make sure that you keep a carbon copy! Write down the date of the mailing: scribble it on the carbon or on a calendar so you can refer to it from time to time. Unless specified otherwise, fillers will not be returned. If you haven't heard from the editor for sixty days, accept the fact that your item has been rejected. Dig up your carbon copy, retype your material, and send it to another publication. It's a good idea when you are searching for markets to list several of them in your little notebook. Then when it's time to try, try again, your second choice is right there and you won't have the task of scouring around for other publications.

Let me emphasize right here that it's imperative that you mail out more than one filler at a time. This is the only way to protect yourself from the barbs of rejection slips. And they do sting! Even the professional writer is not always immune to them. If you make it a point to send out three or four fillers at about the same time, one rejection will not crush you. Later, when you are doing some articles and stories, always have two or three fillers out in the mail. They are easy to do and you will get an acceptance from time to time.

Read the list of markets for fillers in Chapter 11 carefully. Decide which ones sound appropriate for your kind of material. Go to your main library and find some copies of the publications. Get the feel of the magazine or newspaper. Jot down the names and addresses and the managing editor's name or the name of the man or woman who is in charge of the category. If you can't get much information, write "Filler Department" on your envelope. Even that little touch will save the editors some wear and tear as they go through their daily avalanche of mail.

5

Now Try an Article:
Writing from
Personal Experience

Es war einmal ein junger Mann, und dieser Mann war
Kadett an der amerikanischen Militarakademie West Point.
Eines Tages lernte er ein junges Mädchen kennen, das ihm
sehr gefiel. Es dauerte nicht lange, und er war sich daruber
klar, dass dies die rechte Frau fur ihn sei . . .

(German Catholic Digest, 1957)

You have just read the first paragraph of the first article I
ever wrote. After arriving in Germany in the summer of 1956, I met
the editor of the *German Catholic Digest* at a dinner. He asked me
to write my impressions of his country and to describe the life of an
army wife. I was flattered, of course, but I didn't know anything
about article writing. In desperation, I started out by saying that
once upon a time, there was a young man, a cadet at West Point,
who met a young woman he really liked, and they decided to get
married. From that time on, they lived in many parts of the United
States and in Japan. I then went on and told about living in gran-
deur in some places and very simply in others. I discussed in detail
what it was like to live on an army post and described the setup of
military quarters, the commissary, the post exchange, the clubs,
the schools, the recreation facilities, and so on. I eventually added
my five children to the story and told about the hectic move to
Aschaffenburg, Germany. Believe me, it was work! But as I wrote, I
could see my stilted phrases turning into readable material. I even
added some humor. I related the story of a friend of mine who
found herself stranded downtown because of a flat tire. She called
her husband and said she was on Einbahnstrasse near the bakery.
When he roared with laughter she knew she had done it again—a
stranger in a strange land. Einbahnstrasse means "one-way street."
(Even though I could speak the language fairly well there were
times when I too made some faux pas.)

I'll always be grateful to those German editors who started me
on my career in writing. In fact, they also bought my second article,
"Meet My Friend, St. Jude," which had a much more polished lead.

It was inevitable, I suppose, that I write about my first German kaffeeklatsch. In the words of an old TV commercial, I can't believe I ate the whole thing. I still can't believe it, and yet it was twenty-four years ago when I rang the bell of Frau Meyer's house and along with three other American wives stepped into the nineteenth century. A streamlined version of the article reads:

> The next time you "take ten" for a coffee break, give a thought to the American army wives stationed in Germany who are experiencing der Grossvater von all coffee breaks—a real kaffeeklatsch.
>
> American wives are always fascinated by the elaborate ritual of a German coffee party, and they find themselves accepting one invitation after another. But they soon discover, to their great horror, that the extra calories have an insidious way of turning into extra pounds, and they are soon fighting their own private Battle of the Bulge.
>
> I'll never forget my first kaffeeklatsch in the picture-postcard town of Aschaffenburg. Why don't you come with me to 42 Gutwerk Strasse and meet our hostess? You'll see for yourself why this little social event is causing so many problems. . . . Elsa, Frau Meyer's maid, opens the door and ushers us into an old-fashioned parlor. Frau Meyer comes forward to greet us and offers us some butter cookies and a glass of Rhine wine. (It's an afternoon affair.) After an hour of exchanging recipes and discussing topics ranging from politics to children, our hostess slides open the doors to her dining room. The table looks elegant with its Bavarian china and silver candlesticks; we can see that she went to great lengths to make us enjoy our visit.
>
> And here comes Elsa with the first cake. It has a torte dough and is filled with pieces of fresh fruit covered by a gelatin glaze. Take some, but wait for the bowl of Schlag (whipped cream) to head your way. This is the real thing, with only a touch of sugar and vanilla added. One bit of advice—don't try to sneak only a smidgen onto your cake. Frau Meyer will look greatly dismayed and exclaim, "Oh, Mrs. Davis! You need more cream," and then she'll lean over and plop another blob on your portion.
>
> And just as you are finished—in comes the second cake.

It's a chocolate one made from a special recipe that comes from the Black Forest. You can't refuse: you're here to win Brownie points for your country, remember? How about some you-know-what to put on top? And another cup of coffee? Don't look now, but here comes the bowl again.

What? You want to go home? Not yet. Our hostess leads us into a little sitting room and here we must have a glass of apricot liqueur. Make sure you drink every shimmering drop laden with those double-barreled calories. Smile, girl, smile! And deep down inside you have to admit that everything you've had today has been delicious, delightful, and delectable. You'll come back again—just like us.

(American Weekend, March 1958)

In the spring of 1958, we found ourselves on the move again and this time it was to an exciting city 110 miles behind the Iron Curtain: Berlin! I knew I had to write about it and sold the story to *American Weekend* in record time. I called it "Quick, Ma, My Cloak and Dagger!" and described what it was like to move with five children into an area where there was an element of danger. I told about the train ride from Frankfurt and stopping at Marienburg so that the Russians could come aboard and check our passports. It took place in the middle of the night while everyone else was sound asleep. I peered out of the window, but rivers of rain on the glass made it almost impossible to see. This was the checkpoint, and from now on we would be in a Communist world until we reached Berlin. Part of the article read:

As we raced on through the dismal night, I struggled to a sitting position from time to time and tried to catch glimpses of horror and intrigue in the countryside. Toward dawn, I gave up the fight because the rain beat at my window so furiously that I couldn't see a thing.

The next morning at eight o'clock, we gathered our brood and baggage together and set foot in the lovely city of Berlin. We were escorted into an army sedan and whisked away to our German house in the American sector. . . . And so once again, for at least the thirtieth time in eighteen years, I settled down to the challenge of making a house into a home.

(American Weekend, June 1958)

I went on to describe in Mata Hari style how I imagined seeing a spy behind every tree or a Mercedes following me no matter where I went. I was doing it tongue-in-cheek, of course, but I found out later that I was closer to the truth than I'd realized.

As I wrote this article, I made a discovery. A style was beginning to emerge, one that sounded like me. It was helping me to sell my wares; the editors seemed to like it. When I look back on those days of teaching myself how to write, I know now that I was doing the right thing. The only way to learn to write is to write. The only way anyone can develop his own style is to put words to paper.

I was also learning how to write a tantalizing title and to sprinkle my material with anecdotes and quotes. But the next article that I wrote was almost straight narrative because of the subject matter. It was my reaction to Premier Khrushchev's ultimatum of November 27, 1958. He called on the West to sign separate peace treaties with the Federal Republic and East Germany by May 27 of the following year. If they refused to do so, Russia would sign a separate treaty with East Germany and turn over to them the supply lines to the city. The ultimatum came at a time when the weather was cold, wet, and gloomy, and I decided to tell the outside world how we felt behind the Iron Curtain. I never dreamed my article would hit the front page of *American Weekend* and be read throughout Europe. My lead did the trick:

> Frankly, I don't know how much longer I can stand being in the dark. Even though it has only been a matter of ten days since it all began, it seems as though an eternity has gone by . . . Even this old house has lost its charm because there is no longer any laughter echoing throughout its rooms. An air of gloom has settled over all of us and everyone goes silently about his tasks wondering if there will be further complications.
>
> Oh, wait a minute! Do you think I'm talking about the situation here in Berlin? Oh, no! I'm just describing what it's like to have two small boys sick with the measles.
>
> (*American Weekend*, December 1958)

My children did have a bad case of this childhood disease and caused us a great deal of worry. The rest of the article did bring out the fact that the American families were so caught up in everyday living and coping with an epidemic of flu that they had little time to be concerned about world affairs. A few weeks later, I met our commanding general at a party and breathed a sigh of relief when he stared at me—and grinned.

Were all of my articles written overseas? It seems that way, but I have done a number of them much closer to home. You have heard many times "Write about the things you know." It doesn't really matter where you are. Now is the time for you to jot down notes on events in your life that will be of interest to other people.

Students and Their Experiences

Think back. Can you recall an adventure of your own? One of my students told about the time she lived in a haunted house in California. When she moved in with her husband and two children, there was no indication that they had a "house guest." But as soon as she was alone in the house after breakfast, the player piano downstairs in the recreation room began to bang out a tune. She eventually called in a repairman, but he couldn't find anything wrong. She persuaded her husband to move.

Have you ever seen a flying saucer? Another student of mine was driving home one night from a social gathering in a town in New Mexico and saw one cruise past the front of her car. Her husband was with her and saw it, too. He checked with the airlines and military flights the next morning, but nothing had been scheduled at that hour. This experience will stay in her memory forever; it will almost write itself when she turns it into an article. She'll have an effective punchline: her husband had never been a "believer" until then.

Have you survived a divorce? Are you going through one now? While providing a kind of therapy for you, your article may help your readers deal with a traumatic moment in their lives. A friend of mine is still putting the finishing touches to her account of what happened when she decided to leave her husband. It had an extra touch of poignancy about it: she was seventy-six and he was eighty-two. When I discussed the divorce explosion with an acquaintance of mine who is a member of Pen Women, she said that someone should write it from the viewpoint of a parent whose son or daughter is divorcing. She may do it herself. It's happening in her own family and causing emotional problems which should be aired.

Going down Memory Lane can provide you with material that will find a ready market. Nostalgia is quite popular and will be for a long time. Can you tell us what it was like to hear those old radio programs such as "Fibber McGee and Molly," "Pepper Young's Family," "Lights Out," and "The Shadow"? Can you re-create for us the penny candy store? Can you tell us about the games you played years ago? One piece of nostalgia I have found delightful was written by Herb Daniels for his syndicated "Modern Almanac" column. Part of it reads:

Remember how cellars used to be before they became combination saloons, pool parlors and laundries? Dark, cool, damp, earth-smelling, cobwebby, mysterious. And filled with the best eating that's been man's lot since Eve first bit into that apple.

It was at this time of year that the cellar finally came into its own. All the preserving was done. Row on row of Mason jars glinted in the room. In them was distilled rain and sun and not a little of the salty sweat of many a long row hoed in the July blaze.

The cellar was every home's own supermarket. In this storehouse, the tomato was king—whole canned tomatoes, tomato juice, green pickled tomatoes, and that best-smelling, best-tasting gift of the gods—homemade chili sauce. I can taste it now!

There were piccalilli, corn relish, applesauce, mustardy chow-chow (with never enough cauliflower chunks), spicy crabapples, seckel pears with a cinnamon stick to each jar, and grape juice so rich you had to cut it three to one with water. And apple butter. And watermelon rind pickles. And pickled beets. Let's not forget the canned sweet corn and string beans . . .

There weren't any checkout counters at this supermarket. The only thing was you had to watch your step on the rickety stairs and be careful not to bump your head on the top of the

door frame. And hurry, because there was SOMETHING lurking in that far dark corner. I swear it.

("The Modern Almanac," November 8, 1970)

If you've read this and been taken back to your cellar days,
you must admit that you can certainly identify with Herb Daniels's
article. Keep reader identification in mind when you are writing; it
will help you sell your manuscripts. Whenever the reader can nod
his head and say, "That's the way it was" or "Hey, that's what
happened to me!" you're on your way to a sale.

Do you have a pet that gave great meaning to your life?
Florence McConnell, one of my students at Culpepper Garden (a
retirement home in Arlington, Virginia), wrote up a short feature
on her dog Frank (see Appendix). She took us back to the time
when she was a child—about eighty-five years ago—and remem-
bers the family discussing Frank's age and what they should do
about it. Her shaggy, black-and-white dog resolved the problem: he
simply disappeared the next morning, and they found him after the
spring thaw. He had been listening to them on that cold, wintry
night. When she read the story to us, there were tears in our eyes by
the time she finished.

At the present time, a retired army colonel is regaling us with
stories about his parrot named Joe and is getting his material
published in the *Senior Scribes* newsletter. A retired navy man is
working on a story about his Sealyham terrier. That article should
find a home soon in one of the new pet magazines now on the
market.

Do you enjoy meeting people? How about writing a profile on
someone in your neighborhood who should get some recognition?
Muriel McKenna did that very thing: she interviewed ninety-five-
year-old Jack Phillips, another resident of Culpepper Garden. Jack
was a song-and-dance man in New York in the early 1920s and
knew Sophie Tucker and Al Jolson. Even though his eyesight is
now failing, he still entertains at the drop of a hat and is much in
demand at the nursing homes and senior citizen centers in the area.
Muriel's thumbnail sketch was published in the *Senior Scribes*
newsletter.

If you have gone through a traumatic experience, you may
wish to write an article for one of the religious markets. Lois Miller,

a recent student of mine, sold her first article to *Seek,* an adult Sunday school publication always on the lookout for material that will inspire its readers (see Appendix). Lois wanted to share her feelings about what it was like to go through a divorce, but she also wrote about the power of prayer and the solace of verses from the Bible. She added a quote from her father: "We can be sad because of what we don't have, or we can be thankful for what we do have. This is what makes a person happy or unhappy; it depends upon one's perspective."

The only time I slanted an article toward a religious magazine was years ago when my children were small and I was putting them through the third degree to find out who had cut off the cat's whiskers. What made the deed even more dastardly was the fact that only the right side of Tiger's face had been tampered with, making her look particularly ridiculous. What I had in mind was to write something about mothers and how they must face Life with courage and fortitude and patience. But I knew that I needed a peg on which to hang my tale of woe. And it materialized when I attended a church brunch for mothers only a few Sundays later.

The young Irish priest who was the guest speaker told us that we were already on the way to sainthood. His four married sisters and their myriads of children always made him content with his life whenever he paid them a visit. Raising offspring required heroic qualities, the good father said. And he admitted that he always breathed a sigh of relief whenever he left his nephews and nieces. I laughed along with the other women, but as I drove home, I mulled over what he had told us. Why couldn't I become a saint? I decided to give myself a trial run for one whole week.

Monday was uneventful. On Tuesday, I almost picked up the phone to tell Alice what I had heard about Betty. On Wednesday, the car stalled downtown and I swallowed the words I wanted to say. On Thursday, I tripped over Tinker Toys and choked on an expression or two tucked away in my subconscious. On Friday, I began to grumble as I groped under beds for socks and missing items; on Saturday, I smiled a lot; but on Sunday, the dam broke. I was getting ready to go to a formal reception and couldn't find my new pink lipstick. My five-year-old was watching me as I scurried about and bemoaned my loss. Then in a calm voice he said, "It's over there on the windowsill." I ran into the bathroom, grabbed it, applied it, and heard him add, "It fell into the toilet bowl, but I got it out." I froze. But my sense of humor took over and I laughed until I cried. I wrote up my story and sent it to *Ave Maria*, a national publication. Several months later, there it was on the front page of the magazine. Underneath the title "The Time I Almost Became a Saint" was a sketch of a halo a little askew. Later it was also picked up by *Family Digest.*

What would you do if you were given a million dollars? A local retired real estate investor and millionaire recently sponsored an essay contest and was impressed with the answers he received. Milan Herman, one of my students, placed third among 1,300 contributors. The first prize of $1,000 was won by a man who said he would set up a fund for catastrophic situations that couldn't be handled by today's organizations. Milan wrote about developing better self-esteem and said that she would use the money to attack negative thinking. She fully believes "Man is what he thinks"; he can go forward only if he first has a desire for a better life. She used several quotes from Napoleon Hill and W. Clement Stone, whose books have inspired thousands to reach their full potential. Milan didn't receive any money, but this was her first success in the writing field and she now plans to do some articles on a special course she is taking on Alpha mind power. (There is a footnote to this story: the man who sponsored the contest announced that he is going to establish a foundation for catastrophic situations.) If you find yourself wishing that you had the opportunity to win a touch of fame or fortune, look around you—and read your daily newspaper with the eye of a hawk. Pounce on any item that gives you a chance to use your way with words so you can gain the experience you need to become a professional writer.

Are you a jogger? Are you a runner? Are you a soccer player? Editors of new magazines are looking for stories on these three subjects right now. Do you collect dolls or antique cars or matchboxes or presidential campaign badges? Editors of magazines and newspapers are waiting for you to send in short articles on the hobby dear to your heart. Do you like to travel? It doesn't matter whether you go by plane or train or car—someone out there wants to hear about your trip. The travel market has grown fantastically and you should be able to find a home for your manuscript.

The Structure of an Article

If your thoughts have been racing as you read this information, you must be asking yourself how to begin. There is a kind of formula to article writing, and if you master it you will be able to turn out salable material ranging from a 600-word feature to a 2,500-word detailed piece of nonfiction. Every article needs the following:

1. A provocative title
2. A narrative hook or lead
3. An anecdote or a quote (one or more) or some dialogue
4. Good transitional sentences
5. A summary ending

Choose the right title and you'll have an editor grabbing your manuscript the minute he sees it. Here are some of mine:

"Maid in Japan," which told about the wonderful woman who worked for us in the Land of the Rising Sun.

"The Things I've Swallowed for My Country," which described the various foods I've eaten in foreign countries.

"The Year I Saw Stars," which revolved around the famous men and women I interviewed on a radio program.

"Would I Do It Again?," which gave a rundown of my life as an army wife and stated that I would do it all over again if I had the chance.

I've become a title freak and collect them whenever I can. For example, a local TV station presents its weekly monster movie under the title "Creature Feature." A secondhand dress shop not far from here calls itself "The Second Time Around," and a new one close by is known as "Once Is Not Enough." A current book on genealogy written by Suzanne Hilton is called *Who Do You Think You Are?* When I started my course in writing fifteen years ago, I decided to call it "Write Now!" and I honestly believe that it's what motivated a number of people to sign up. If you find that you're having trouble coming up with a title, try creating one with alliteration. Two or three words that begin with the same letter sound pleasant to the inner ear: *The Wind in the Willows*, *Loon Lake*, and *Little Lord Fauntleroy* are good examples of this kind of heading.

Of all the aspects involved in writing an article, the most important is the *narrative hook*. It should "hook" the reader into wanting to read on and enjoy or learn from the item in front of him. You will have to experiment and find out which lead suits you best. There are five I especially recommend:

1. **The anecdote.** This one will tell a little story:
   Tom Bingham discovered the secret in the attic one rainy morning when he awoke before his wife and had little to do. He decided to investigate a loose spot of wallpaper where he had become convinced that a mysterious secret door lay hidden.
2. **The comparison.** This one usually compares two things:
   While the search is on again for the Abominable Snowman, there is another species of the human race which deserves attention. She is known as the Army Wife.
3. **The question.** This lead should be provocative:
   Did you know that sixty thousand wives ran away from home last year?
4. **A quote.** This lead can come from a famous person or an authority on the subject you're writing about:
   "Never put off until tomorrow what should be done today," Thomas Jefferson said many years ago.
5. **A startling fact.** This narrative hook should make the reader sit up and take notice:
   If you should visit the British Museum in London one of these days, you would, no doubt, be impressed with the mummified body of an Egyptian woman more than five thousand years old. But what would really make an impact is the fact that her fingernails are painted a dark red.

When you have chosen your lead, you are ready for your second paragraph. It should set the scene and give the reader an idea as to what the article is all about. The end of the article should be a summary of what you have been saying. If you find yourself floundering and becoming long-winded at this point, take a look at your second paragraph and "play it again, Sam," but use different words. And make it short and sweet; don't let your endings drag on and on.

And what comes in between? If your article is a mini one, you could get by with one quote or anecdote. But if it is more than 1,200 words, sprinkle it with several. These little touches add backbone and authority to your material. Suppose you were writing about goals in life and how important they are. You could use a quote from Abraham Lincoln: "I will study and prepare myself, and then, someday, my chance will come." Or you could use a line from Shakespeare: "What's brave, what's noble, let's do it!"

If your article is more than 1,500 words, it is a good idea to send a *query letter* to an editor. Put your best foot forward by catching his attention at the beginning with an intriguing item from your manuscript. Make sure you send a self-addressed stamped envelope (SASE)—and don't be surprised to get a go-ahead from the publication you're aiming for. If this kind of letter writing is causing a furrow in your brow, take heart. There will be a sample in the next chapter for you to digest.

6

Now Try an Article:
The Research Piece

Not too long ago, the phone rang and an editor of the *Army Times* said, "How would you like to do an article on tipping for our upcoming travel supplement?" I paused—and agreed before I could think.

Later, as I did some routine things around the house, I muttered to myself as it dawned on me that what I knew about tipping could be said in one sentence. Waiters expect 15 percent of the bill and hairdressers about the same. How could I ever put together 1,500 words for Ruth? The answer, of course, was to ask my traveling friends and to do some research.

But when I checked with some of the people I knew who seemed to be always flitting from coast to coast, they were surprisingly vague. They finally admitted that most of the time they overtipped because they didn't know how much to give. There certainly is a need for this kind of article, I thought. And once again I was impressed with editors and their uncanny knack of knowing what the public needs.

The next day, I trekked down to my neighborhood library and asked the woman at the desk if she had any suggestions about how to find some facts on tipping. She agreed with me that the card files under "T" wouldn't help at all, but told me to take a look at the compact edition of the Oxford English Dictionary. Its two volumes contain all the words one would find in the original thirteen volumes, printed in microscopic type; it comes equipped with a magnifying glass. Making like Sherlock Holmes, I turned to the right page and peered down at the fine print. I could make out that the word "tipping" was used in several books written in the seventeenth century, but I couldn't understand much more. I put on my reading glasses, and even they didn't help. I finally went home with a new Fodor book on travel and an old book on etiquette. The travel book supplied me with some basic guidelines on tipping in the United States, but the one on social behavior gave me a much broader base from which to work. It covered my subject from planes to trains to cruises to hotels and nightclubs, including bellboys, doormen, barbers, and beauticians. But I had a problem. I needed more up-to-date information.

One of the women in my class saved the day. She came in one morning with an article from a recent issue of *Travel & Leisure*. It featured tipping do's and don't's for the United States, and was just what I needed. But there was one more thing I had to unearth: how did the custom of tipping get started?

I called the reference librarian at the main library and she managed to find the answer in a book called *A Book about a Thousand Things* by George Stimpson. I trudged down to Central to read the material for myself and could hardly put the book down. But I jotted down the details and dashed out the door, eager to get started on a challenging writing project.

That spring, my article, "Timely Tips on Tipping," appeared, and part of it looked like this:

> Your bags are packed. Your travel arrangements have been checked and rechecked and you're rarin' to go. But once again there is a cloud on the horizon that threatens to spoil your trip. How much should you tip and who should receive the gratuity?
>
> Relax. Stop muttering and accept the fact that the quaint old custom of tipping is here to stay. And it *is* old and quaint. According to historians, it all started three centuries ago in London.
>
> The story is told that it was customary in those days to have boxes in English inns and coffee houses for the receipt of coins for the benefit of waiters. "To Insure Promptness" was printed on the boxes to remind guests that a coin deposited inside would bring excellent results in the way of special service. Sometimes, the phrase was abbreviated to T.I.P. To this day, the British don't realize what a Pandora's box they created so innocently in the 17th century.
>
> *(Army Times,* May 1980)

The rest of the article was done alphabetically, starting with "Airlines" and ending with "Trains." I saved a special tidbit for my ending (many writers use this device):

> And after reading all of these details on tipping, you may be tempted to sign up for the first space shuttle flight to an-

other planet. You won't have to travel that far. You can plan a
trip to China, where tipping is unacceptable and even considered rude.

Some Results of Research

Several of my students did quite well when they ventured out
into the research field. Lila Parker, a retired government worker,
was determined to get published and succeeded with a short feature we all found delightful. She followed the basic format of
article writing and combined research with her own knowledge of
her subject. What did she write about? Tea! That was her title—
perhaps she could have improved upon it, but for her first attempt,
she did remarkably well. See for yourself. Her feature in its entirety reads:

When Peggy Teeters suggested to her writing class that we
try our hand at writing a short feature, I knew I'd have to put
the kettle on as well as my thinking cap. Tea is such a mystical,
delightful brew with such special powers. Its magic has been
believed and sought for ages.

The ancients believed that tea brewed from the sage leaf
added vigor and joy to living and it was thought by many to be
the path to immortality. At one time, it was a favorite tea in
China. Why not try it? You may find it's your cup of tea. Put
two teaspoons of sage leaves in your favorite pot, add boiling
water, and let steep until it becomes a pleasing, deep color.
Fresh sage tea is especially invigorating when you feel
"achey" and miserable from a cold.

Dill makes a good tea, believed by many, my grandmother
included, to be a tranquilizer. A cup of dill tea sipped before
retiring was considered one of Mother Nature's non-narcotic
sleeping aids. Put 1/8 teaspoon dill seed per cup into an
earthenware pot, add boiling water, and steep until flavor and
strength is to your liking. The word "dill" is derived from the
word "dillian," meaning soothe or lull. So after a day when
everything and everybody seem to have been working against
you, it may be just the thing to soothe, quiet, or lull you into
peaceful sleep.

Rose hip tea is available in health food stores, and is packed with vitamin C. If you are ambitious, you can make your own. Those red seed pods on your rose bushes called "rose hips" are loaded with ascorbic acid (vitamin C). During World War II, England harvested two hundred tons of rose hips from roadsides and gardens and used them to replace citrus fruit. (Three rose hips equal one orange in ascorbic acid.) To make a nourishing, nutritious tea, gather your rose hips and wash well. Cut off and discard the seeds, dry them in a slow oven for a short period, pulverize them, and brew them for tea. It's quite a chore, but the tea will be your own.

Sassafras tea, brewed from the leaves of the sassafras tree, was used as a spring tonic in my grandmother's day. The Indians enjoyed a tea made from the sap of the tamarack tree, and I remember a tea made from spruce gum—and who hasn't added a fresh or dried mint to the teapot for that fresh minty flavor? Many exotic teas are available in the gourmet section of many stores: jasmine, orange pekoe, spice, mint, English, Chinese, etc. There is a tea for every occasion and every individual taste preference.

Eugene Field's grandmother, in his "Grandmother's Prayer," prayed for a needle in her hand when she got to Heaven so she could mend the little boy angel's breeches, remember? But for me:

"I pray that, risen from the dead,
    I may in Glory stand;
A crown, perhaps, upon my head
    But a teacup in my hand."

(*Arlington News,* January 1976)

Another student broke into research when she became curious about a huge bird she spotted every time she traveled to the Eastern shore in Maryland where she had a summer home. It looked like an eagle—but not quite. She interviewed a native of the area and found out it was an osprey, a large bird of prey of the hawk family that spent its winters in South America and returned to the tidewater areas of Maryland and Virginia in March. This gigantic bird signaled the coming of spring. My student was especially intrigued by its towering, umbrella-sized nest resting on telephone-pole crossbars. She pointed it out to me when I traveled with her one day, and told me she had already asked the editor of the *Baltimore Sun* if he would like her to do a story about her find. He was more than interested. And so it was that Dody Smith sold her first article to a newspaper editor who wanted to give some good news to his readers.

During the past several years, Muriel McKenna, a student of mine at Culpepper Garden, has sold several research articles. One of them was about the history of gloves; she listed about thirty-five facts regarding them that made interesting reading. Another one gave details on the beetle of ancient Egypt, explaining how it became idolized by the people (see Appendix). She brought out the fact that the beetle or scarab is popular even today as a motif in jewelry design. Both items were published in the *Arlington News*.

Historical Articles

Nan Carroll, a history buff, did some research on the Declaration of Independence and wrote about the many places in which it had been hidden since its signing. Whenever war threatened, it was moved to a safe place, including a linen sack in a barn in 1814 and in a vault at Fort Knox in 1941. Her story was published by the *Virginia Cardinal*, a regional magazine noted for its informative articles.

My own research into the history field has led to a number of sales. One I'll never forget was accepted by a TV magazine published by a station in California. It featured the life of Elizabeth I and served as an introduction or lead-in to the TV series "Elizabeth R." I'll never try anything like that again. I read so many books on the Virgin Queen that I'll be an authority on her for years to come. But I did like my lead:

> In the turbulent era of the 1970s, studies are constantly being made to evaluate the impact violence makes on the lives of small children. In the year 1536, the mother of a three-year-old girl was beheaded on the command of her father, and since that time, psychologists are still trying to understand its full significance.
>
> (*Gambit*, February 1972)

Another historical article I researched made me an expert on the life of Libbie Custer, the wife of General George Custer, who was killed in the Battle of the Little Big Horn. Mrs. Custer kept a diary for many years, and her account of her life with the army wagon train in the Dakota and Montana territories makes fascinating reading. She survived blizzards, droughts, windstorms, and Indian attacks, but never lost her spirit or courage—until the afternoon of June 25, in 1876. She had a premonition that something terrible was going to happen to her husband and his men, who had been ordered to round up the Sioux and Cheyenne Indians and bring them onto reservations. She had never felt that way before. Ten days later, word came that the soldiers had been massacred at the time she had experienced a feeling of doom.

Ideas for Research

Here are some ideas for research that should prove to be challenging and fun for you to do:

> • The *Titanic* has finally been found. According to reliable reports, the original copy of "The Rubaiyat of Omar Khayyam" was on board. Why? Where was it going? Who had bought it?

> • King Arthur is alive and well and living in Cornwall, England—or so the legend says. He will come to his country's rescue whenever he is needed. Was there ever a King Arthur or a Merlin?

> • What are the ten books that changed the world?

> • What grows between the roots of pine, oak, or willow trees? Why, the truffle, of course. What is a truffle? Did you know that truffles can be found in California around Santa Rosa?

> • Is Noah's Ark on Mount Ararat? What do the aerial photos show? What is the latest word from the expedition?

• Did you know that shoes were so important in the early life of man that they were given magical powers—and that they once were used as money and food?

• Did you know that there is a phantom ship that sails the Hudson River? Is it the *Flying Dutchman* finding a port at last; or Henry Hudson's *Half Moon* looking for its captain; or Captain Kidd coming back for his treasure?

• Have you heard of the Chalice of Nanteos in Wales? It is supposed to be the cup used by Christ at the Last Supper. It has been on exhibit at Nanteos House every summer for many years, and people from all over the world have come to see it. But a short time ago, the woman who owned the house and chalice simply vanished. What happened? And where is the fragile, olive-wood bowl today?

• How would you like to take a college course, talk to a friend, and visit your doctor—without leaving your living room? It's happening now through communications satellites.

• Christopher Columbus discovered America, but he also came across the pineapple, the green turtle, and what other foods?

• Why are there blue-eyed Indians in the Carolinas? Could they be descendants of the "Lost Colony"?

• Did you know that popcorn was the first "puffed" breakfast cereal eaten by our early settlers? And that the Iroquois Indians made popcorn soup?

• What is folklore? How much of it is true?

• Have you ever heard of the Baker Street Irregu-

lithic monuments such as the Pyramids and Stone-
henge?

• Are you an authority on roses? In addition to telling amateurs to plant them as early as possible in the
spring, why don't you also inform them that fossilized
rose petals 35 million years old have been found in
Oregon and Montana; George Washington was our
first rose breeder; and James Brady, a White House
gardener, developed the American Beauty during
Grant's administration.

• Why do Canadians feed their cats very well on
Christmas Eve? What special event takes place in Germany on December 6? Who created the first crèche?

• Who are the three VIP ghosts in the White House
and who has seen them?

• Do you suffer from Ozmania? Many people do—
and they enjoy every minute of it: they are admirers of
L. Frank Baum, who wrote the fourteen Oz books, and
they flock every year to the convention held in Castle
Park, Michigan. Who was this man? How did he become such a storyteller?

Time to Begin

Now that you have some subject matter to research and write
about, what should be your next move? Since you are a beginning
writer, choose a topic in which you have some expertise or interest.
After you choose your article idea, jot down some important points
and develop them into a blueprint or outline. This preliminary
work will also help you write a more convincing query letter later
on. (Make sure that your query is well-thought-out and not just a
half-baked idea.)

Now begin to fill in this framework from your knowledge, and
then browse through your encyclopedias for more information.
But don't stop here. Go down to the library and see what new

books and articles have been written on your subject. This is also the time to check *Books in Print* in case there are several publications on the subject not available at your library. The *Readers' Guide to Periodical Literature*, of course, will tell you what articles have been written about your topic. If there is an expert in the field living in your area, set up an interview with him. Later, add these bits of new information to what you have on hand. And now comes a very important part of article writing: read through what you have written or typed and ferret out an intriguing item. Use it for the lead in your query letter.

Let's suppose you have decided to write about the VIP ghosts at 1600 Pennsylvania Avenue, Washington, D.C. You live nearby and plan to contact Lillian Parks, who coauthored *My Thirty Years Backstairs at the White House*. What publications should you aim for? Why not try a new magazine for children called *Cobblestone* and mention to the editor that it would make a different Halloween story for their October issue? If you have this in mind, remember that you should send seasonal material at least six months ahead of time for magazines and about five weeks for newspapers. This means, of course, that your query must go out several weeks before those deadlines. (You'll find more details about this procedure in the chapter on markets.)

The Query Letter

And now, at last, you're ready to write that letter. First of all, try to find out the name of the current editor of the magazine or newspaper to whom you plan to send your article. You can do this in several ways. Look at the publication's masthead, which lists the names of the staff members; try to find the articles editor, if possible. If you have trouble finding the person who is in charge of the section you're aiming for, call and ask the personnel office. You can also go through a current copy of *The Writer* or *Writer's Digest* and look through the article markets written up in detail. Each one will contain the name of the editor and what she is looking for. *Writer's Market*, an annual directory, is a good source for editors' names in the article field, but you may want to check the magazines for possible updates. If all else fails and you can't find out the name of the person in charge, simply say "Dear Editor."

Type your query single-spaced and have it cover about a page. Do your usual heading and then say:

> Dear Editor,
>
> Did you know that the White House has ghosts? Don't visualize run-of-the-mill spirits, however; these are VIPs who have played an important role in history. What is especially amazing is the fact that they have been seen by down-to-earth, reliable people.
>
> Would you like to see a 1,500-word article about the ghosts of Abraham Lincoln, Dolley Madison, and Abigail Adams and where they make their appearances? I plan to describe what happened when they were seen and why the rumor is growing that our President's home is definitely haunted.
>
> In the course of my research, I have been in contact with Lillian Parks, the coauthor of *My Thirty Years Backstairs at the White House*. She is providing me with some details that will add a special touch to my story.
>
> I'm an elementary school teacher who knows that young people are always intrigued by ghosts in any shape or form. Frankly, so am I!
>
> Sincerely yours,

As your credits grow, you can mention toward the end of your letter the fact that you have sold some articles or stories. It's a good idea to state that you have studied the format of the publication; you should do this in every category of writing. If you become familiar with the magazine or newspaper, you'll know if your style of writing fits in with the editor's needs.

Send out your query with a self-addressed stamped envelope. You should receive an answer in two or three weeks. If it's positive, whip your article into shape. Make sure you have a tantalizing title; a narrative hook bound to whet the appetite of your reader; a second paragraph that sets the scene; a sprinkling of anecdotes or quotes or some dialogue; and a summary kind of ending or one that adds a special zing to your subject.

Fold your manuscript into a white No. 10 envelope and make sure you enclose a SASE. If your article is more than five pages, it's a wise idea to mail it flat accompanied by a thin piece of cardboard in a 9x12 envelope. Always keep a carbon and record the mailing date. When two months have gone by, send a polite note to the editor to find out what has happened to your submission.

If photography is your hobby, get into the habit of mailing some 5x7 black-and-white glossies with your manuscripts. You'll be able to sell to some of the slick magazines and make more money. If you don't know one end of the camera from the other, you can obtain pictures free or for a nominal sum from public relations departments, government offices, the Library of Congress, and the National Archives. Other sources are listed in *The Writer's Resource Guide*, published by Writer's Digest Books. (This book is a boon to all article writers because it lists hundreds of organizations that supply free information on all kinds of subjects.) Remember, however, that you will be able to sell your material without photographs; I've been doing so for many years.

A footnote: The moment your manuscript has hit the sack at the post office, get those mental wheels turning again and come up with another idea to work on. Don't sit and wait for word from the editor. A professional writer goes on to bigger and better things immediately.

7

....

Fun with Fiction:
The Juvenile Scene

It may sound strange, but one of the best things that ever happened to me in my writing career involved a rejection slip. It took place years ago when I returned from a two-year stint in Kyoto, Japan. I had soaked up so many fascinating details about the country that I simply had to tell Americans all about it. I decided to write a children's story, something I had never done before.

In fact, I had never written any fiction until then. But I sat myself down and scribbled away. My protagonist was a nine-year-old-boy named Yozo; I described his lifestyle, which was so very different from ours. I told about his sleeping on a *futon* (quilt) instead of a bed; eating a breakfast of rice and fish; keeping a cricket for a pet; and eating all of his meals seated on the floor in front of a low table. My story revolved around a big event in Yozo's life: he was going to play a violin solo at the concert that was being given for the American schoolchildren. I really thought I had a winner and sent it off to *Children's Activities*, a well-known magazine at that time.

I wasn't prepared for its return. But clipped to the rejection slip was a note from the editor which said: "I enjoyed reading your story about Yozo, but it isn't actually a story. You must take that little boy and give him a problem . . . a dilemma of some kind that will resolve itself at the end. After you have made the revision, send your manuscript back to me."

I'll never forget that editor. She gave me my first lesson in fiction writing. After much thought, I did give Yozo a problem. I decided to make him meet with an accident on his way to school—nothing serious, but it caused him misery in several ways. He was daydreaming as he pedaled along on his bike and didn't see an army truck coming around the bend. It hit him and off he flew into some scraggly bushes. He wasn't hurt, but his only set of clothes was torn and muddy. The two soldiers were deeply concerned and offered to drive him to school because his bike was slightly damaged. On the way, Yozo told them about the concert, and that now he wouldn't be able to play his solo. It was too late to go home—and anyway, he didn't have any other good clothes.

When Yozo arrived at school, his teacher was upset, and told him that she would have to ask Misa to fill in for him. Yozo was crushed and went off to get himself cleaned up. His parents would be so disappointed . . . but a few minutes later, his teacher came running down the hall with a big box addressed to him. Yozo tore it open and found some new clothes and a note from the soldiers saying that they hoped they'd fit and that he would be able to play his solo. It all ended happily, and Yozo was a big success.

This whole story sounds so contrived—and of course it was. But there must have been something about it that appealed to the editor, because it was published a few months later. Here are the first few paragraphs:

> Yozo seemed to hear a voice calling him from far away. He slowly opened his eyes, and there stood his mother with his clothes over her arm.
>
> "Wake up, Yozo! Wake up!" she was saying.
>
> Yozo thought a second. Then he jumped up from his bed on the floor.
>
> "Today is the day! Today is the day!" he cried. "Where is my breakfast? Are those my new clothes?"
>
> "Not so fast, my young son," his mother said, smiling at him. "Go put your bed away in the closet as you do on other mornings. There is still time for that."
>
> Yozo folded his quilts and went over to the closet. He pushed open the sliding door, put the quilts inside, and shut the door again. Now the bedroom had become the living room.
>
> (Children's Activities, March 1956)

I must admit that I found the whole process of creating a story rewarding and exciting. I also discovered that it took time to develop a plot and believable characters. During the next ten years, I devoted nearly every waking moment to raising our family and moving to various army posts and towns. When I did have a minute to myself, I wrote a personal article giving my reaction to a situation. It was easier and less time-consuming.

My second fiction story, "A New Home in Germany," was published by Golden Magazine in 1968. This time I had two protagonists, a brother and sister who had to live in a foreign country for three years. The plot, less contrived than my first one, centered around Jimmie and Jo-Anne trying to earn enough money to send for their collie who had to stay on their uncle's farm. (Any child who has had to leave a pet behind could identify with the story.) Some of the following excerpts will show how I developed the plot:

> Jimmie woke up very suddenly—his head had just banged against something that clanked.
>
> "Ouch!" he exclaimed, and wondered what had made that rattling sound. He turned over to go to sleep again when all at once he thought of something. His bed at home had never sounded like that! And then he remembered. He wasn't back in his room in Maplewood; he was on a ship headed for Germany. His head had banged against the metal guardrail which kept him from falling out of the top bunk in the stateroom.
>
> Jimmie's dad was a colonel in the army. He had been ordered to work in West Germany for three years. Colonel Anderson was now on his way to his assignment with Mrs. Anderson, Jimmie, and Jo-Anne.
>
> Jimmie and his sister, however, weren't too happy about leaving their friends back in Maplewood, Wisconsin. But what made them most unhappy was the fact that they had to leave Laddie, their beloved collie. A week before sailing time, he had been hit by a car. He was now at the vet's and would be there for three or four more weeks.
>
> "Dad," Jo-Anne had asked as they went up the gangplank the day before, "when will we see Laddie again? Would it cost lots of money to send him over when the vet says he's all better?"
>
> "It would cost quite a bit," Colonel Anderson answered. "But aside from the money, I think Laddie will be happier on Uncle Joe's farm where he can help herd the cows."
>
> . . . Finally, at ten o'clock that night, the wild storm quieted down. Later, as Jimmie tried to get to sleep, he thought, "I bet PeeWee's never been in a hurricane! Wait till I write and tell him about it!" PeeWee was his best friend back in Maplewood.

And then he thought of something else. The more he
thought about it, the more excited he became. "Say, wouldn't
that be something," he said out loud. "Maybe I can get some
money that way. I'm going to do it right now."

(*Golden Magazine*, May 1968)

The editors used this part of the story as a cliff-hanger; their
readers would have to buy the June issue to see what Jimmie was
planning to do. My story was 4,000 words long, so they also realized that that length would discourage a juvenile from following
the storyline to the end. And so "A New Home in Germany" became a two-part serial with a certain element of suspense.

In June the readers found out that Jimmie had written a story
about his trip on the *U.S.S. Patch* and had sent it to a contest in a
magazine. A few weeks later, after they had settled down in Wurz-
burg, Germany, he received a letter telling him that he had won a
prize of $20. This was the beginning for a plan to get Laddie sent
over to them. From that moment on, Jimmie and Jo-Anne did
chores; struggled to get A's in school; hoarded their weekly allowance; saved any money sent to them by grandparents, etc. But
when they tallied it up, they could see that it wasn't enough. They
were sure they needed at least $75. If they could come up with that
much money, their father would realize how much they wanted
Laddie with them. But how could they earn some more?

By this time, I had run out of ideas myself, but I was also
determined to get Laddie overseas. And then help came from an
unexpected source. One of my sons came home from a school trip
to Heidelberg Castle and gave a glowing account of its halls and
dungeons and legends. I immediately sent the Anderson family on
a sight-seeing trip to the castle. So? How would that add to Jimmie
and Jo-Anne's little nest egg? Aha! I had a scheme that would do
the trick. As the Andersons followed the tour guide, Jimmie wan-
dered off and found himself in one of the dungeons. He couldn't
believe what he saw: a frail old man on a torture rack! He eventually learns that a movie is being made and is asked to play a bit
role. You already know the ending, right?

Because the story was already so long, I added a hurricane, the
sighting of a white whale, some German phrases and customs, and
getting lost in the castle. I also had to be careful that these things

didn't interfere with the flow of the story.

I must also mention the fact that the artwork for both stories added a great deal; the first one had black-and-white sketches and the second had full-page color pictures of Jimmie, Jo-Anne, and Laddie. If you are an artist, query the editor before you mail out sketches with your manuscript; most publications hire their own illustrators and pay them separately.

As you read my stories, you probably noticed that boys seemed to dominate the scene. Since I had had four sons in a row, it seemed more natural to write about them, for I knew what made them tick. But in the 1980s, many editors want to see girls playing the lead role.

If you have always wanted to write fiction for children, beat a path to the library now and immerse yourself in the wealth of material you'll find there. This is the only way you can prepare yourself for the juvenile market. It seems to be changing constantly—and you will have to make a decision. You can write in the traditional vein or give your protagonist one of the current problems involving drugs, alcohol, sex, divorce, and minorities. If you have always wanted to write about dragons and fantasy, charge right ahead. If your story is good, it will also find a home in the marketplace.

The Age Groups

While these thoughts are swirling around in your head, decide which age group you'd like to write for. There are five to choose from:

- three to six: the picture-book crowd.
- six to eight: the beginning reader.
- eight to twelve: the easiest age group to write for.
- twelve to fifteen: the most difficult group.
- the reluctant reader . . . fairly new and includes every age.

If you would like to write for the three-to-six age group, be aware that your story or text must complement the pictures. Your manuscript supplies half of the book; the artist does the rest of it.

Also take into consideration that your young readers have a short attention span. Don't get bogged down with detail, and keep your sentences short and your words simple. And once again, start your story with an intriguing tidbit that will make that little boy or girl eager to turn the page.

What should you write about? Tell a story about a cowboy, a clown, a rabbit, a dog, a kitten, a caterpillar, a horse, a cow, a chicken, a bear, a kangaroo, or a witch. They have all been used in books during the past few years and have earned a spot on the library shelf. You could even do a simple mystery. Right now there is a preschooler book at my library called *The Mystery of the Red Mitten* by Steven Kellogg. It is aimed toward the two-year-old child. For the first time in library history, books for that tender age are now finding their way into the juvenile section to be read aloud at bedtime.

The ingenuity of the writers for this age group amazes me. Recently, they came up with the idea of using the "scratch and sniff" technique (invented by advertisers) in a number of books. Have you seen—and sniffed—the one about the smells of Christmas? The author made sure to include the wonderful fragrances of pine, gingerbread, and candy canes. Another one I enjoyed was a mystery which could be solved only by sniffing the clues on each page.

If you want to try a picture book some day, make sure to use repetition in your story. Young children like to read words or phrases over and over again. Reread your battered copy of *The Wind in the Willows* by Kenneth Grahame (read it aloud), and enjoy such lines as "So he scraped and scratched and scrabbled and scrooged and then he scrooged again and scrabbled and scratched and scraped . . ." One word of caution: writing for this age group looks easy, but the men and women who create these books admit they work on each one for a long, long time. They suggest that anyone entering this field spend many hours at the library.

Has Dr. Seuss always been one of your favorite authors? His early attempts at writing should encourage you to try, try again if your book ideas are turned down at first. His first manuscript, *And to Think That I Saw It on Mulberry Street,* was rejected by twenty publishers before his big break came. Theodor Geisel (his real name) says that he was planning to burn his manuscript when he happened to run into an old college friend he hadn't seen for some time. He was surprised when he learned that he was now the children's book editor for Vanguard Press. Geisel mentioned the story he had written, showed it to the interested editor—and Dr. Seuss was born. Since that time, his books have sold eighty million copies in this country alone, and he has even won international fame with his Loraxes, Drum-Tummied Snumms, and Grinches.

If you're interested in doing a book for the six-to-eight age group, you're hitting a mushrooming market. The next time you go to the library, look for the "beginning reader" section and take some books home. You'll find material on science, famous people, American history, animals, and even grammar, all written in a way that appeals to the young reader. And of course you'll also come across books of adventure and mystery and everyday happenings which capture the imagination of youngsters learning to read.

A mystery that has done well in this age category is *The Secret Three* written by Mildred Myrick and published by Harper & Row in 1964. It is still popular, and I know why. It revolves around secret codes, messages in bottles, and three boys who form a secret club. Mildred joined one of my writing classes not too long ago, and is now working on a story about a boy ghost who didn't want to wear white. I asked her where she found the idea for her successful story, and she told me that during the years she had been a librarian she had observed what appealed to boys who were six, seven, and eight.

Before attempting to do this kind of story, it is important that you become familiar with the format. There are only a few words to each line so that the beginning reader is not intimidated in any way. Here is a passage from *The Secret Three*:

> Mark came to stay with Billy
> at the beach.
> "Let's go for a swim,"
> said Mark.
> "We have to wait an hour
> after we eat," said Billy.
> "Let's take a walk on the beach.
> The tide was high this morning.
> We may find something good
> on the sand."

If you're planning to try the eight-to-twelve age group, you'll be working in the category that is the easiest to do. The majority of the books in the children's section at your library are for this age span. They cover all kinds of subjects: sports, school, mystery, adventure, fantasy, legends, ghost tales, life in foreign lands, folk tales, and family living. But other topics are finding their way into this age level, and you'll find books on divorce, ethnic problems, and other social issues. If you lean more toward realistic fiction, read the books written by Judy Blume, who has achieved great success in this field. But no matter which direction you go, make sure that your protagonist is a year or two older than the age level you're shooting for. This holds true for all of the age groups I've mentioned except the little picture-book people.

In the early-teens age group, girls are interested in gothics, career stories, mysteries, and light romance, including boy-girl relationships at school. Boys seem to prefer sports, outdoor adventure, mysteries, and space, including science fiction. There is a dearth of material for these readers. The eight-to-twelve age is easier to please because of their burgeoning curiosity, but young teenagers are in the midst of finding their own identity, and their reading tastes change from day to day.

Do you remember what you were reading at this stage in your life when you were neither fish nor fowl? If Nancy Drew or the Hardy Boys pop into your mind, you'll be happy to hear that they are still being read today. They seem to be an integral part of growing up, even though they are not literary masterpieces. Harriet Stratemeyer Adams is the author of both series, and manages to turn out a new Nancy Drew every year. (Mrs. Adams is now in her eighties.)

Writing for the reluctant reader is another trend in children's fiction that is gaining momentum. These "hi-lo" books are a challenge to write because they must intrigue the reader at once, but contain a limited vocabulary. During the past four years, I have written stories about Nathan Hale, Columbus, Jules Verne, Mary Shelley, and Robert Louis Stevenson using this "hi-lo" approach, and sold them to an educational publisher who is interested in the reluctant reader. When I wrote my two-page sketches of these famous men and women, I knew I would have to reach out and grab my reader before he realized what had happened. Here are three of my narrative hooks:

Mary Shelley jumped up in bed, her eyes filled with terror. She had just seen a man-like monster brought to life! Was it real? Was she dreaming? She looked over at her husband, who was sound asleep, and felt better. There was nothing to worry about.

But when she finally dozed off, the ghastly figure came back again! . . .

When Robert Louis Stevenson was forty-one years old, he did a very strange thing. He gave away his birthday.

Step into your time machine and travel back to the 15th century. You are on a small sailing vessel in the middle of the Sea of Darkness. This sea is really a part of the great Atlantic Ocean. No one has ever been here before.

These stories, of course, were a combination of fact and fiction, but based on thorough research. I had to be careful not to stretch my imagination beyond a certain point or I would be distorting history or the life of a well-known figure.

Try Magazines First

While most of this chapter has emphasized children's *books*, I advise you to try the magazines first. Your chances of getting a byline are much greater if you begin here and save that book idea until next year. That doesn't mean that you shouldn't cram your little notebook with storylines whenever they pique your imagination. Hang on to them; their time will come. But in the meantime, become familiar with *Cricket, Highlights for Children, Horn Book, Ranger Rick, Boys' Life,* and *Child Life*. If you would like to see a complete list of juvenile publications, including religious magazines, check an April issue of *The Writer;* it also publishes a book list every July. You can also get all kinds of information from *Writer's Market,* compiled by Writer's Digest Books, and *The Writer's Handbook,* put out by *The Writer.*

If you decide to go into magazine writing, the age groups of your audience will be comparable to the ones discussed earlier in this chapter. My two stories on Japan and Germany, for example, fall into the eight-to-twelve age range. I enjoy working at this level;

you may find that this group of youngsters is the one you need for the stories you have in mind. And if you're wondering whether this kind of writing will bring you a nice little check from time to time, I can tell you that the pay will vary from $20 or $30 up to $150. In fact, my two-part serial on Germany brought me a $300 check, the most I have ever received for a children's story.

But whether you choose to write a story for the magazines or for the book market, you will be working with characters, plots, settings, and dialogue—all the necessary ingredients of fiction. If you have always been vague about how to put a story together, it all boils down to this formula: Come up with an interesting protagonist; give him a problem to solve; confront him with several obstacles, usually one big and one or two small; and then have your hero or heroine figure out a solution.

One of the best ways to prepare yourself for writing for the juvenile market is to read some of the books recommended by eminent people in the field. At the present time, Virginia Polytechnic Institute sponsors an organization called the Children's Literature Association, which consists of teachers, librarians, authors, parents, and publishers. The six hundred members are trying to encourage serious scholarship and research into the area of children's literature. In 1976, they published the names of the ten books they considered to be the best during the past two hundred years. See how many you know.

1. *Charlotte's Web* by E.B. White
2. *Where the Wild Things Are* by Maurice Sendak
3. *The Adventures of Tom Sawyer* by Mark Twain
4. *The Adventures of Huckleberry Finn* by Mark Twain
5. *Little Women* by Louisa May Alcott
6. *Little House in the Big Woods* by Laura Ingalls Wilder
7. *Johnny Tremaine* by Esther Forbes
8. *The Wizard of Oz* by L. Frank Baum
9. *Little House on the Prairie* by Laura Ingalls Wilder
10. *Island of the Blue Dolphins* by Scott O'Dell

There is another list of books that you should be familiar with, and this one has to do with the Newbery Medal Awards given each year for an outstanding children's book. John Newbery (1713-1767) was an English publisher and bookseller, and the first person to print and sell books for children. The award was created in 1921 by Frederic Melcher, chairman of the board of the R.R. Bowker Company, publishers of *Library Journal* and *Publishers Weekly*. It is presented every year by the Children's Services Division of the American Library Association. Ask your librarian for the list of winners or check into your own set of encyclopedia at home. In the meantime, here are eleven of them that are particularly popular with boys and girls at my local library:

> *The Voyages of Dr. Doolittle* by Hugh Lofting (1923)
> *The Cat Who Went to Heaven* by Elizabeth Coatsworth (1931)
> *Caddie Woodlawn* by Carol Ryrie Brink (1935)
> *Call It Courage* by Armstrong Sperry (1940)
> *The Twenty-One Balloons* by William du Bois (1948)
> *Ginger Pye* by Eleanor Estes (1952)
> *Island of the Blue Dolphins* by Scott O'Dell (1961)
> *A Wrinkle in Time* by Madeleine L'Engle (1963)
> *From the Mixed-Up Files of Mrs. Basil E. Frankweiler* by E.M. Konigsburg (1968)
> *Summer of the Swans* by Betsy Byars (1971)
> *The Grey King* by Susan Cooper (1976)

The time may come when you can add your name to this select list of authors. Don't scoff. Many of these men and women didn't dream it could happen to them. If you have a story to tell—do it now!

8

Fun with Fiction:
For Adults Only

> The white-haired matron in the elegant black suit stepped
> gingerly over the body and disappeared down the hall.

Please read this statement carefully. Find some notepaper and
jot down the first thought that comes into your head. What was it?
Was it the location? Did it involve the woman? Or the body? Can
you picture the scene in your mind's eye? Good!

Now give a name to that white-haired matron . . . Now set the
scene somewhere . . . Now describe the body lying on the hall
floor. What do you think happened? Let your imagination run wild
and write about 200 words. If you have never tried to do fiction
before, you may be pleasantly surprised to discover that you have
a flair for this kind of writing.

During the past five or six years, I have given this premise to
all of my classes to introduce them to fiction. The students usually
reacted in the same way: they could never come up with a plot—
never. A week later, many of them came into class with a big grin
and admitted that someone else seemed to take over their pencil or
typewriter, and with a vengeance. As I had each one read his story,
I sat and listened in amazement: they had become so bloodthirsty!
In fact, they surprised themselves with their creative ideas concerning the matron in the elegant black suit. Here are a few excerpts from their tales of terror:

> The white-haired matron in the elegant black suit stepped
> gingerly over the body and disappeared down the hall. I had
> come down the stairs just in time to see her slip her gun into
> her black bag and almost run to the nearest exit. Her victim lay
> in a spreading pool of blood. I ran outside and saw a blue van
> drive away. I memorized the license number—JAK214—and
> saw that it was from Ohio. I then raced over to an outside
> telephone and called the police, telling them what had hap-
> pened and where the murder had taken place. They appeared
> in about five minutes, but when I met them at the door, I had to
> tell them that the body had disappeared! . . .

It was 1952 in New York City and it was the middle of February. It was cold and heavily overcast. In the old Beverly Arms Apartment on Riverside Drive, the surviving ceiling light on the fourth floor hung valiantly doing its best to illuminate the area without help from the broken fixture that matched it.

The door of Room 411 opened quietly and closed quietly. Emerging was the handsome, heavily built Mrs. George Concannon dressed in an elegant black suit. Her white hair was beautifully groomed. She was fifty-two, and Mr. George Concannon was dead.

Being somewhat of a mixer and loving to dance, Edwina had emerged at her usual time for dancing at 9 p.m. There was a small dilemma for her on this night, however, when she encountered the body in the hall, but she solved it with characteristic expediency. She stepped over the body of a man whom she assumed to be dead. After all, it was none of her affair . . .

The white-haired matron in the elegant black suit stepped gingerly over the body and disappeared down the hall.

"Cut!" yelled the director. "We've got to do this scene again. Take your places and make it believable this time!" . . .

The white-haired woman in the elegant black uniform stepped gingerly over the body and disappeared down the passageway toward the control room.

The starship's automatic cleaning and maintenance system, sensing the inert mass in the passageway, clicked open a concealed cell door from which emerged a humming maintenance robot. The robot, a service-proven Model R2D2B, activated its forklift members, picked up the sweatsuit-clad body, and carried it to the short-term storage unit. . . .

Captain Marshall frowned as she stepped from the passageway into the control room. The senior watch officer, Commander George Smith, hurried over to greet her.

"Good morning, Captain. Have you rested well?"

"Good morning. Yes, yes—fine. How are we proceeding?"

"Everything in order, ma'am," replied the commander.

"We've made up four of the seven hours we lost in the comet cluster yesterday. Should be back on schedule by the end of the watch. Otherwise, all systems are normal, and we are cruising routinely."

The frown returned to Captain Marshall's brow. "Commander Smith," she said, "I was just attacked in front of my quarters by an escapee from the cargo cages . . . "

The white-haired matron in the elegant black suit stepped gingerly over the body and disappeared down the dimly lit hall. No mail again today. She turned her key to open her apartment for what she knew would be the last time . . .

In addition to these unexpected reactions to my simple statement, I must tell you that the "body" was also pictured by my students as a rat, a mouse, and a mannequin. The students all agreed that it had been a fun assignment; some said they planned to stay in the fiction field for a while and try a short story or two on their own.

Why write fiction? The number one reason, without a doubt, is the fantastic money you can make if you have a hit. Aside from that, you'll like the idea of transporting your readers to another time, another place, and creating characters that are exclusively your own. Remember, however, that fiction writing is more difficult than nonfiction, and you will have to learn some of the techniques used by the professionals. But the thrill you'll derive from dreaming up plots and characters and dialogue will far outweigh the effort involved in any learning you'll have to do.

The desire to tell stories and to listen to them is inherent in all human nature, and the art of storytelling is probably the oldest of the arts. Egyptian tombs of six thousand years ago contain domestic and social tales inscribed in papyri, and down through the corridors of time, the Greeks, Romans, Persians—all the peoples of the world—have contributed fables, legends, and earthy stories. The tales from the Arabian Nights, consisting of two hundred stories, came from Persia, India, Mesopotamia, or Egypt; no one knows for sure. But one thing is certain: they enhanced the art of telling a story. And Bible scholars are quick to point out that this holy book is the repository of every conceivable kind of short story.

In our own country, this literary form came into being at the beginning of the nineteenth century. Edgar Allan Poe is considered the father of the American short story and he describes it in this fashion in his "Review of Nathaniel Hawthorne's Twice-Told Tales":

> A skilful literary artist has constructed a tale. If wise, he has not fashioned his thought to accommodate his incidents; but having conceived, with deliberate care, a certain unique or single effect to be brought out, he then invents such incidents as may best aid him in establishing this preconceived effect.

Since that time, writers of short stories have emphasized the importance of creating a single effect, and that this kind of fiction can be compared to a portrait in miniature. It's all there, but it's compressed into an economical size. Anyone who decides to go this route must realize that he cannot do much embroidering of his characters or plot; he must constantly be on guard to shape his subject matter to get his desired effect.

Parts of a Short Story

The elements of a short story are:

1. Character
2. Plot
3. Setting
4. Style, point of view, tone, mood, atmosphere, and other factors in the telling of the story.
5. Theme
6. Symbolism

The first three elements shouldn't give you any trouble, but let's clarify the others.

Style means the selection and arrangement of words and sentences. It's the way in which a thing is said.

Point of view means the relation of the storyteller to the story.

Tone means the author's attitude toward his material.

Mood refers to the attitude of the characters in a story toward what is happening.

Atmosphere refers to the general emotional effect of a scene from a story.

Theme means a brief statement of the meaning of the story—the author's message. For example, "The grass is always greener on the other side of the fence," "Revenge is sweet," or "All that glitters is not gold."

Symbolism in a story emphasizes meaning on another level. In other words, are the images literal and limited to concrete experience or do they suggest values and beliefs and ideas?

And now that your lesson is over, let's take a look at a formula for writing a short story:

Character(s) ⟶ problem ⟶ complications ⟶ climax ⟶ solution

A character or characters are introduced. They meet a problem. The situation becomes more complicated and finally reaches the climactic point of tension. Then the decision is made, the problem is resolved, and the story is brought to a close.

The problem faced by the character along with its complications is called the "rising action"; the solution or denouement is called the "falling action." Take a look at this diagram so that you can see the action of a short story more clearly:

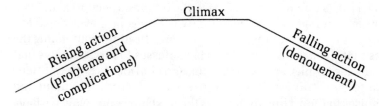

Study the diagram again. Notice the length of the lines. You can see that the "Climax" line is the shortest of the three. When you write your story, keep these proportions in mind.

Probably the best way to tell you how a short story is written is to choose a classic and analyze it using the above formula. If you've never read James Thurber's "The Catbird Seat" (first published in *The New Yorker*, November 14, 1942) you're in for a treat. The story begins:

> Mr. Martin bought the pack of Camels on Monday night in the most crowded store on Broadway. It was theatre time and

seven or eight men were buying cigarettes. The clerk didn't
even glance at Mr. Martin, who put the pack in his overcoat
pocket and went out. If any of the staff at F&S had seen him
buy the cigarettes, they would have been astonished, for it was
generally known that Mr. Martin did not smoke, and never
had. No one saw him.

Now that the hero, or protagonist, has been introduced, we
need a problem. As we read more of the story, we find out that a
Mrs. Ulgine Barrows has come into the firm and is unsettling
everybody with her determination to make various departments
more efficient; she has, in fact, caused several people to lose their
jobs. Rumor has it that she is getting ready to invade Mr. Martin's
private domain and do away with some of his files. Mr. Martin
decides that the only way to stop her is to rub her out. (Now
we have a story going, but we need more of a plot.)

He goes to her apartment one night intent upon murdering her
with a weapon he'll find there, but to his great dismay, he can't find
any. He could use the poker or andirons, but he doesn't want to
make the murder that bloody. (Now our story shows the *complica-
tion.*) What can he do? All of a sudden, a wild idea comes into his
head. He sits down with brash Mrs. Barrows and accepts a highball
from her and smokes a cigarette, two things he never does. Mr.
Martin now schemes to get Mrs. Barrows fired by convincing the
boss that she has lost her mind. He confesses to Mrs. Barrows that
he smokes, drinks, and takes heroin, and confides to her a fictitious
plan to bump off Mr. Fitweiler, the boss. She orders him out and
promises to report him to the boss the next morning. (Now we have
the *crisis* of the story.) When she tells Mr. Fitweiler about Mr.
Martin's smoking, drinking, and threatened violence, this sounds
so ridiculously out of character for the file clerk that Fitweiler
thinks she needs psychiatric care and fires her. Mr. Martin returns
to his beloved filing department, where he will once again be in the
catbird seat. (This is the *climax* of the story.)

I should note that the title comes from a baseball term refer-
ring to a batter with three balls and no strikes against him, and
means sitting pretty. I should also mention to all of you amateur
detectives out there that Mr. Martin bought Camel cigarettes to use
as a red herring after he had rubbed out Mrs. Barrows. She smoked

only Luckies; he planned to puff a few puffs after the murder and then leave his Camel cigarette in the ashtray with hers. He never dreamed he wouldn't be able to find a weapon!

This **plot** can be described as one in which the hero accomplishes his goal through his own efforts. There are six or seven other basic plots often used in magazine stories, but your first attempt should revolve around the one I've discussed. If you become serious about short story writing, you may want to buy a book called *The Thirty-six Dramatic Situations* by George Polti, published by *The Writer.* I also recommend a paperback called *Fifty Great Short Stories,* edited by Milton Crane and published by Bantam Books. In his preface, Mr. Crane gives his definition of what makes a short story great: "the sudden unforgettable revelation of character, the vision of a world through another's eyes, the glimpse of truth, and the capture of a moment in time."

If you are determined to write in the fiction field, be aware that whether you do a story or a novel, there are three universal **themes:** man against man, man against nature, and man against himself. The first one is used the most, of course, and is the easiest to write. The third is psychological and requires a special kind of insight into the thoughts and desires of the protagonist.

Suppose you are all set to start your story. Will you tell it in the first person? In the third? Or will you create an omniscient observer who knows what the characters are thinking in addition to what they are doing? No matter which **point of view** you choose, stick with it; your reader won't appreciate your shifting about. Hemingway did a remarkable job with a mixed point of view in "A Clean, Well-Lighted Place," but he was a master at his craft.

Now that you have chosen your own point of view (third person would be a good one to start with), let's choose a **character.** Let's give him some traits. How? Most writers do a composite of themselves, borrowing one or two traits from a friend or relative. Instead, why not use the signs of the zodiac? Your character could be one of the following:

Scorpio. She is fascinated by religion, drugs, and sex. She can be either god or demon.

Libra. He has a compulsion to be fair and can see all sides to all questions; is also intelligent and gullible.

Taurus. She is tranquil, passive, resists change.

Leo. He is proud, loves luxury, attention, ease. He rises easily to fame—unless arrogance or flattery drags him down.

Sagittarius. He is innocent, filled with charisma, an idealist.

Remember that when you are creating your imaginary people you must give them a balance; every human being is composed of good and bad characteristics. Your story will ring more true if your hero acts like the rest of us.

How long should your story be? It can range from 1,500 to 10,000 words, with an average length of 5,000. You can see that in this limited form it is impossible to become philosophical in theme or carry out an elaborate plot. It's the economy of the short story that makes it such a challenge to a writer: to stay within bounds and yet produce a great piece of fiction.

Have you ever thought of writing a short-short? These run about 1,500 words and are ideal for those of you who can't spend too much time at the typewriter. But don't picture it as a sketch or a vignette; it contains all of the elements of the regular short story: the opening, introduction of the problem, intensification of the conflict, the crisis, and the resolution. But you will have to cut down on your descriptions and dialogue and use succinct phrases instead of paragraphs to get necessary information across.

This kind of writing isn't a breeze, so start now to read some magazines that feature a short-short from time to time. You'll soon get the feel of it and see how quickly the author gets into the story, and how he makes you believe that it conveys the same impact as a full-length short story. If you are successful at this type of fiction, you can expect a check for $750 or more from some of the slick magazines.

As you get ready to write your story of adventure or love or mystery or horror or science fiction, here are several other helpful hints:

1. When you begin your story, introduce your character, setting, and problem in the first few paragraphs. Your reader wants to know what is going on as soon as possible. Most of the writers of today conform to this rule; get into the habit of doing so with your stories.

2. Your dialogue should move the plot forward;

that means your characters should make statements that fill us in a bit more on the storyline or the people in the story.

3. Try to find a title for your story that fits. What famous novel started out with these working titles?

Tomorrow Is Another Day
Ba! Ba! Black Sheep
Tote the Weary Load
Not in Our Stars
Milestones
Bugles Sang True
Jettison

Have you come up with an answer? You may not believe it, but these were the tentative titles of *Gone with the Wind*.

4. Make sure you do an outline or a framework for your story.

5. Make sure you have a theme.

6. Make sure the story contains a conflict.

7. The reader should care about your lead character.

8. Your story should give the reader an emotional experience.

9. Your story should not contain too many coincidences.

10. Has something changed in your story? If your character or characters are still the same, you don't have a story.

Suppose you have read all of this material and yet you dream of writing a novel. Should you do it? A better question is, *Can* you do it? From what I have gathered, it is easier to write a novel than a short story, but don't believe for one minute that it is simply a matter of adding more characters and a greatly expanded plot. Not so! Writing a novel can be compared to creating scenes in a movie; each one gives dramatic information through the characters. That means, of course, that you will know your characters inside out; you'll know what they think and do and why they act the way they do. It may be work, but it can also be fun. Take a look at this excerpt from an article written by Patricia Harrison, a local freelancer working on her first novel, a mystery:

> I locked the bathroom door, sat down on the edge of the tub and began to type:
>
>> The sun glowed like a melon . . .
>> Like the yolk of an ostrich egg . . .
>> The sun yolked its way screaming into dawn.
>
> "Mom," a small voice yelled through the keyhole, "Why are you typing in the bathroom?"
>
> "It's the only room in this house with a lock on the door, that's why. Just give me a few more hours and I promise I'll come out."
>
> "That's super weird, Mom. Typing in the bathroom. Really weird."
>
> "Thanks for the vote of confidence, kid. Now . . . just let me experience this weirdness for maybe one, two hours, tops, and I'll emerge from these tiled walls with a tome in my hand."
>
> "You're talking funny, too," she mumbled, padding off.
>
> I stuffed the keyhole with toilet tissue and continued:
>
>> She lifted one long, perfect ~~finger leg~~ eyebrow
>> and threw back her ~~thigh~~ head, chortling mania-
>> cally but not without compassion. She had never
>> seen the sun yolk its way into dawn before . . .
>>   (*Washington Post*, December, 1979)

Of course this is a spoof on writing a novel, but if you ever get involved in doing a fast-paced mystery story, you'll find yourself creating descriptions that come close to the ones above. If you keep at it, though, one day you'll see such improvement that you'll be spurred on to finish your book.

Let me emphasize that the **mystery** or detective story is highly structured and not something you can whip off on a rainy afternoon. You always have to tie up every loose end or your readers will pounce on what you have neglected to cover. If you are determined to write in this field, however, read the authors you admire the most and buy a book or two from the publishers of *The Writer* or *Writer's Digest*. You will need some guidelines.

You may want to write some historical fiction. If you are a history buff, you'll find yourself enjoying the research and then weaving it into story form. I've always been interested in the Civil War and decided one day to delve into the lives of Jeb and Flora Stuart, an army couple who deeply loved each other and refused to let anything interfere with their devotion to each other. I was amazed at the intriguing details I uncovered and knew that I had to write a short story about Jeb Stuart, the Confederate cavalry general, and Flora, his young wife, whose father fought in the Union army. I called it "Moment of Decision" and the first two paragraphs read:

> Flora awoke with a sudden start. There it was again—the strange tapping noise she had heard the night before. But this time she was determined to do something about it instead of cowering under the blanket and praying for dawn to come. After all, she had been left in charge of two-year-old Flora and the hired girl, and they were her responsibility.
>
> As she groped in the dark for her red woolen robe and warm, furry moccasins, she murmured, "Oh, Stuart, when are you coming home? I can't stand being alone like this!" But she knew in her own heart and soul that many days and weeks of winter would pass before Lt. Jeb Stuart would return to Fort Riley from his special assignment in Colorado. Even the fact that the new baby was due any day couldn't bring him home any sooner than March or April.
>
> *(Arlington News*, Feb. 18, 1973)

You may want to try writing a romantic novel of suspense. The **gothic** tale is one of the oldest of the mystery forms and is as popular today as it was in the late eighteenth and early nineteenth centuries. The most dominant characteristic of a gothic is the atmosphere. Unlike the harshly realistic world of the private eye, these stories are built on moods and tensions. It is more of a psychological than physical brand of story. For example, there is rarely a description of a violent act; instead, the emphasis is on the threat of violence or the menace of impending danger. The setting and tone of the story serve to make the action of secondary importance. The real suspense comes from being inside an eerie castle where the floor creaks at night, the servants are intimidating, and the handsome host seems to brood over some dark secret.

But wait a minute. Can't a gothic have other settings? Of course it can. Jeanne Hines, a friend of mine, wrote her first tale of romantic suspense set in an old mansion in West Virginia. It was said at Braithwaite Hall that when bagpipes sounded in the night, evil was in the air and death was near. Who would be the next victim? Jeanne called her story *The Slashed Portrait* (Dell Publishers) and has written three more gothics since then.

Another friend of mine wrote her first gothic after returning to the United States from a stay of several years in England. She and her family had stayed in a 250-year-old Queen Anne farmhouse that made a perfect setting for her story. Lanora Miller called her novel *Quickthorn*, and it was published by Ace paperbacks. They told her they hoped she would do some more tales of suspense and romance. Since that time, she has written several others, and pointed out to me that one of the stories took place in the Middle West; gothics do not always have to be in exotic places.

Both of these writers have encouraged me to try my hand at this kind of writing. I'm working on it, but I don't dare to aim for the adult audience yet. I've compromised by slanting my story toward teenage girls who are reluctant readers; there is a definite need for novels of this kind to motivate students to read. I've called if *The Secret of Kellerman Castle*. The story takes place in Virginia, and then in the Black Forest in Germany. I've done synopses of twelve chapters, and in a way, I've written the book. It's too trite and not good enough to send off, but it's been a joy to write—and a challenge. In order to create that mood of imminent danger and impending doom, I had to choose words that would send a shiver down the reader's spine. I started out in the third person but switched to the first so that my seventeen-year-old protagonist, Katie O'Connor, could react more emotionally to her summer at Kellerman Castle. Here is my first paragraph (Katie is in Virginia):

> It's raining. An hour ago it was only a drizzle, but now a storm is brewing. The rain is coming down in torrents, and the wind is rattling the front door demanding to come in. The lights are flickering off and on. There was a time when I shivered in delight in this kind of atmosphere—but not any more. It

only reminds me of last summer . . . a summer filled with
mystery and terror. I know I will never enjoy a storm again.

I hope this teaser will motivate some of you to do a story or
novel as soon as possible. Steal a bit of time from your many
activities so you can try this kind of writing. Creating a piece of
fiction will transport you from a mundane world into one where
characters created from your imagination can work wonders.

9

Of Course You
Can Do a Column

Years ago when Heloise Cruse, an Air Force wife, moved to Hawaii, she found time on her hands and decided to look for a part-time job. In the back of her mind, she toyed around with the idea of writing a column for the *Honolulu Advertiser* devoted to household hints she had picked up from her own experiences. The editor told her politely that he wasn't interested. Undaunted, Heloise asked him several more times, and he finally agreed to hire her and pay her $10 a week for "Hints from Heloise." The rest is history: In three years' time, the *Honolulu Advertiser's* circulation went from 46,000 to 71,000. A few years later, Heloise's column appeared in syndication in over five hundred newspapers. She went on to write several books, and received many awards for her clever domestic ideas. According to reliable sources, she eventually earned $100,000 a year—and to think it all started with a weekly column! When she died a few years ago, her daughter took over, and "Hints from Heloise" is still going strong.

Abigail Van Buren and her sister, Ann Landers, started their columns because they were concerned about the many problems faced by young and old alike. They never dreamed that their advice would take off like a skyrocket and make them known on a national and international level. At first their columns were simple, with suggestions on how to cope with routine, everyday problems, but in later years, they discussed a variety of sensitive subjects with guidelines from clergymen, doctors, lawyers, counselors, psychiatrists, and even economists. In fact, Ann Landers wrote a book in 1978 called *The Ann Landers Encyclopedia.* It covered subjects ranging from abortion to zoonosis, a disease man can acquire from animals. When she started doing her column for the *Chicago Sun-Times* in 1955, she didn't realize how popular it would be and that many readers would take her sage advice—and chuckle over the foibles of humanity. Both sisters write with a sense of humor which seems to temper the grim realities presented in many of the letters.

The name Erma Bombeck evokes a lightheartedness that brightens every nook and cranny. I'm sure her column, "At Wit's

End," was created as a defense against the drudgery of everyday tasks and raising a family in suburbia. It began in 1964, and one year later it went into syndication. Several years later, she decided to put her columns into a book. It did so well that she did five more, including the number one bestseller, *If Life Is a Bowl of Cherries, What Am I Doing in the Pits?* At the present time, her column appears in eight hundred newspapers.

Art Buchwald started out working for an American newspaper while living in Paris. He, too, didn't have an inkling that he would eventually win world recognition for his column and from his books, all written with the kind of wit that tickles our funnybone. I'll never forget one of his columns written in 1974 that told about his taking to heart President Ford's pronouncement that we all had to bite the bullet on the economy. He decided to go down to his local sporting goods store and buy a bullet as soon as possible. But when he told the clerk what he wanted, the man said, "You mean a box of bullets." Art Buchwald told him that one would be enough. This conversation followed:

> "What kind of bullet do you want?"
> "I don't know. Are there different kinds?"
> "Of course. What kind of gun do you have?" he asked.
> "I don't have a gun," I said.
> "Then what do you want a bullet for?"
> "I want to bite on it," I admitted sheepishly.
> (*Los Angeles Times* Syndicate, 1974)

The rest of the column was just as hilarious as the beginning—only a master of his craft could make a serious subject so amusing. Humor, by the way, is the most difficult kind of writing to do, and very few men and women have succeeded in this field.

Are you interested in food and cooking? You don't have to be a Julia Child or a Craig Claiborne to establish yourself as a columnist in this category. A friend of mine by the name of Jane Mengenhauser can vouch for that. Jane had worked on the staff of several newspapers, and had written features on food for the *Washington Post* as a freelancer, but hoped some day to do a column on recipes and cooking. Several years ago, she heard that the *Alexandria* (Va.) *Journal* was looking for reporters. She took six sample columns on food into the editor's office and convinced him to hire her as a columnist instead. Since that time, the circulation has mushroomed and there are five *Journal* newspapers in the suburbs of Virginia and Maryland. Jane is now the editor of the food page, but still does her column. Here are some excerpts from her "Kitchen Sampler":

> Sometimes the little gifts found in the Christmas stocking turn out to be more appealing than a big impressive gift in fancy wrapping.
>
> It's possible that a big and expensive book written by a famous author might not be as useful to you as a collection of cooking and kitchen coping hints. As small as they are, they could make your life a lot easier in the months to come.
>
> So here's a stockingful of kitchen hints and bits of information that I hope will be helpful to you:
>
> Bleu cheese is imported from France. Blue cheese is a domestic product. Gorgonzola cheese is similar to bleu or blue but its homeland is Italy.
>
> For a new rice treat, brown the rice in a bit of butter just until it is golden. Add a dash of white wine and then add the cooking liquid and cook.
>
> Don't suffer from vegetable boredom. Mix peas and cauliflower, green beans and corn, corn and tomatoes, peas and celery . . .
>
> (*Journal* Newspapers, December 23, 1980)

Can a novice ever become a columnist? It's elementary, my dear Watson. There isn't one of you out there reading this book who doesn't have some expertise on some subject. Your best bet is to query an editor of a weekly newspaper, and send him five or six columns running about 350 words each. Also add a rundown of some other aspects of your subject that you plan to do later on. (You must convince the editor that you won't bog down after writing up some of your thoughts and ideas.) Don't expect to do all of your columns off the top of your head; go to the library for more information and angles. Choose a catchy title if you can. And this is the time to scour the writers' magazines for new publications in need of ideas for columns. Your life as a columnist could begin tomorrow—well, almost.

My first column materialized when I'd returned to the States

and was living in Arlington, Virginia. After two years in Japan and
three in Germany, I felt there was a need for service wives overseas
to know what was going on back home. I queried John Wiant, an
editor with *American Weekend*, and he thought I had a good idea.
It was then that "Back Home" came into being. One of my first
columns said:

> For the first time in trading stamp history, a bona fide
> airplane was recently traded for three million stamps col-
> lected by ninety-nine women pilots, all members of a club
> here in the States. They don't intend to keep the plane for
> themselves but have donated it to a Korean club member who
> is planning to teach flying to the women in her country.
>
> Many Americans are installing sauna baths and gym
> equipment in their basements, and the entire family is getting
> into the act of keeping fit . . .
>
> As for some of the other things Americans are doing
> lately, take a look at this—visiting art galleries, rereading the
> classics, setting the dinner table the European way, dancing
> the Bossa Nova, writing their memoirs, learning foreign folk
> dances, and taking art lessons . . .
>
> (*American Weekend*, March 6, 1963)

This weekly column traveled all over the world, and seemed to
be fairly well received. I wrote it for about a year and a half, and it
gave me my most important lesson in writing: self-discipline. Neither rain nor sleet nor a toothache nor a sore toe could interfere
with my meeting a deadline. One of the nicest compliments I got
came from an army officer I bumped into one day after he had
returned from an assignment in Korea. He told me that the minute
he got a copy of the paper he turned to my column, even though it
was slanted toward a feminine world.

After I stopped writing my column, I discovered that I missed
sitting down at the typewriter and telling my readers what was
new in America. Why couldn't I do the same kind of thing for the
women who were not overseas? This time, however, I didn't know
any stateside editor, but I did have a contact with the man who ran
a small advertising newspaper in the Arlington area. D.J. Arone
agreed to hire me on a trial basis, and asked me to do a weekly

column along the lines of what I had done for the *American Week-end*. For the next thirteen years, I turned out one column a week for the *Arlington News* and learned what a deadline was really like. The discipline I had acquired from my first column was nothing compared to that necessary to produce almost seven hundred of them. I soon became expert in the fields of fashion, food, TV, movies, books, cooking, biography, travel, household hints, and famous women. But "The Woman's Side" eventually changed in format when an enterprising associate editor came to work on the paper and suggested that I use a different theme every week. At first, I balked at the idea of changing something that seemed to be doing very well, but the more I thought about it, the more I agreed it was worth a try.

A short time later, my column was called "A Woman's World," and featured a different topic every week. Let me state right here that I found it much more difficult to do. If you can remember what it was like to develop a theme in your English class, you can sympathize with me when I learned that in addition to selecting a topic, I also had to take my facts and mold them into a polished piece of work. I really had to put my creative abilities on the line . . . week after week after week.

Of course it was the best thing that ever could have happened to me. Those early years of column writing had only made me a great researcher; those later years transformed me into a writer. I somehow managed to write about such things as: recipes from Peg Bracken's *I Hate To Cook Book*, which included her famous Stay-abed Stew, a tasty concoction thrown together and into a slow oven while the cook catches up on her reading; how to pretend you've been to the Cordon Bleu cooking school in Paris by adding tarragon to your scrambled eggs or a bit of brandy to your pumpkin pie or some savory to your meatloaf; how to cut your food bill by shopping after a meal, leaving your husband at home, making a list, using coupons, and checking the ads; and paying heed to Julia Child's suggestion to use your senses when you go to the store and snap the beans, pop the peapods, rub the cabbage leaves, etc.

Before you get the impression that my column was centered only around food, I also did material on the history of fashion; the new trends in education; how to lose pounds and keep them off; how to become a successful speaker; how to write effective publicity for your club; how to get unusual program ideas if you've been elected chairman; the pros and cons of watching TV; how to fight depression during the holiday season; the thrill of visiting Lion Country Safari near Richmond, Virginia, and peering at the wild animals through your (closed) car windows; what it was like to wine and dine during Roman times; the curse of the legendary Hope diamond; and how to choose the right kind of clothing to complement your figure.

From time to time, I featured a column on household hints. Why? Because my women readers told me that they enjoyed reading them, and many of them said they cut them out and taped them to the refrigerator door. Here are five I especially like:

- Straight pins will go through material more easily if you use a cake of soap as a pincushion.
- Water rings in fabric will disappear if rubbed gently with a silver spoon or coin.
- Milk of magnesia will take the itch out of poison-ivy-infected skin.
- To prevent dripping fat from flaring up and ruining a steak or chicken when barbecuing, place lettuce leaves over the hot coals.
- Nail polish remover can be used to clean the type on a typewriter. It will not harm the metal and dries instantly.

If you reread the last few pages covering my column ideas, you'll realize that I have mentioned topics that could be written by many would-be columnists. Once you become established with a newspaper and an editor, you'll be allowed more leeway in what you can write about, and you may even find that you will be allowed to do an occasional straight piece of journalism. Begin to beat the bushes now for a weekly newspaper that may be interested in what you have to offer.

Some Topics to Consider

Just in case you haven't found a subject that is your cup of tea, here is a list of fifty topics that might be more to your liking:

Advice	Armchair Travels
Antiques	Astrology

Bridge	It's a Fact!
Car Care	Knit One, Purl Two
Child Care	Know Your Wines
Club Notes	Miniatures
Coin Collecting	Movies
Collectibles	News for Women
Commentary	Nostalgia
Cooking Tips	Nutrition
Down on the Farm	Over 40
Education	Pet Care
Elderhostel Programs	Plant Care
Financial Advice	Politics
Footnotes to History	Radio
Freebies	Religion
Gardening	Retirement Hints
Golden Age	Sewing
Gourmet the Easy Way	Shopper's Guide
Handicrafts	Social Activities
Health	Sports
Hooked on Books	Stamp Collecting
Household Repairs	Theater
Humor	Travel Tips
Idea Exchange	TV

Syndication

When you've found your niche on some local publication, you may want to try getting syndicated. Warning: it won't happen overnight. You can query the following:

- Copley News Service, PO Box 190, 591 Camino de la Reina, San Diego, CA 92110. Interested in newspaper columns, puzzles, cartoons, and comic strips. Submit sample of column with query. Include SASE. Reporting time: one week. Photocopies OK.

- Creative Communications, Division of Creative Enterprises, Box 377, Centreville, VA 22020. Wants weekly columns on self-improvement, politics, health, nutrition, ecology, and consumer interest. Prefers columns of 500 words or less.

• King Features Syndicate, 235 E. 45th St., New
York, NY 10017. Looking for newspaper columns only.
Submit cover letter along with samples and enclose
SASE.

These are only three of the syndicates now in existence. If you
become serious about getting syndicated, look for a book called
Syndicated Columnists by Richard Weiner which will give you
profiles of the major syndicate companies along with hundreds of
syndicated columns for you to study. Also write to *Editor & Publisher*, at 850 Third Ave., New York, NY 10022, and ask about their
syndicate directory. You can get more details from *Writer's Market* and *The Writer's Handbook*.

As for payment, authors can receive 40 to 60 percent of the
gross proceeds, but some syndicates pay the writer a salary or buy
material outright.

Getting Started

As soon as an idea for a column begins to perk in your mind,
write down the various aspects of it immediately. Don't let those
thoughts slip away. Let's suppose that you are going to write about
cooking, a subject in which you have some expertise. Aside from
sharing a number of delicious and unusual recipes with your
readers, what else can you offer? Since most editors expect you to
send them five or six sample columns, you'll have to produce a
variety of things to talk about.

This is the time to use your ingenuity. One of your sample
columns could tell the story of Apicius, the Roman gourmet who
wrote the first cookbook almost two thousand years ago. Another
could discuss the free cookbooks available from certain processed-
food distributors. Another could feature a typical dinner served at
Mount Vernon by the Washingtons. Two or three could highlight
cooking shortcuts and facts on proper nutrition. You can also give
advice on microwave cooking.

With these samples on hand, you should be able to convince
the editor of a weekly newspaper that you can communicate with a
readership for a long time. Many people like to read about food
even if they make every effort to stay out of the kitchen. Mention

that fact to the editor, and you may find yourself hired.

Then what? After your column takes off, make plans to extend its publication. If your weekly circulates in a limited area, you can reach out to other newspapers in the state. Send them half a dozen tearsheets (samples of your column taken directly from the paper), with a cover letter. You can find a list of newspapers in the *Editor & Publisher Yearbook* or *Working Press of the Nation* at your main library; they will also give you the circulation, editor's name, and other vital facts. Make sure to send SASE with your query.

Later, when you think it's time to try a syndicate, go through the same process. Once again tell the editor what you have in mind and why his readers would be interested in your material. But this time you'll have an edge: your published columns will add credibility to your qualifications.

After doing a column for fifteen years for local publications, I can assure you it is one of the most rewarding types of writing. You'll be asked to speak at luncheons; you'll receive fan mail; and you'll be invited to many social gatherings. And best of all, you'll see your writing become more professional and act as a stepping stone to other creative ideas.

10

It Could Fill a Book

An idea for a book was practically handed to me one Sunday afternoon in the summer of 1961 when I attended a reception at Fort Benning, Georgia, for new officers and their wives. Many of the young women I met confessed they were a bit bewildered by the strange new world they had entered, and wished they had a guidebook that could explain army life in a simple fashion. They told me that the book they were using overwhelmed them with its detailed instructions. Couldn't I come up with an easy, breezy version that would explain the etiquette and protocol and yet make army life sound like fun?

I didn't give them a direct answer at the time, but a few days later when my friend Thelma Brown stopped in to see me (we were both living on the post), I found myself saying, "Thelma! How would you like to write an army-wife handbook with me?" Thelma was the Auntie Mame type, always bubbling over with wit and enthusiasm. We both liked the army and had given all kinds of programs for the Officers' Wives Club in the States and also overseas.

She agreed in a flash, and I filled her in on what had happened at the Sunday reception. Then both of us sat on the porch steps of my house, grinning like Cheshire cats and dreaming about the fame and fortune that awaited us around the bend. We didn't dare say out loud that we didn't have the foggiest notion of how to put a book together.

We met several times during the next week and made an outline of what every young army wife should know but was afraid to ask. We would do a preface together, but we would divide up the ten chapters. What chapters? We had subject titles, but that was it. We did have a name for the book that I thought would do nicely: *This Is the Army, Mrs. Jones.* Maybe this takeoff on a popular tune would catch the fancy of the military wives everywhere.

When we finally sat ourselves down to put word to paper, we soon learned that it was one thing to write skits and doggerel for luncheons, but quite another to describe and explain army life. But we believed so much in what we were doing—and knew there was a need for it—that we kept on until we had five chapters finished.

At this point, we thought it was time to approach a publisher or two, and found that our friends and relatives had no ready contacts. Finally, we went over to see someone on post who worked in public relations and who gave us the names of two places in New York City. I sent off two letters explaining our little project, but in both instances the answer was a flat no. Thelma and I refused to quit, and the day came when a company in Charlotte, North Carolina, took us on. We couldn't believe it—somebody was willing to gamble that we could write a successful book!

And then it happened. Thelma's husband received orders to go to Paris within a few short weeks. We vowed that we would do the book by mail; nothing could stop us now. Thelma sent me material so that I could put it all together and make the publisher happy with the results. After almost two years of work, the galleys came in the mail and I knew that *This Is the Army, Mrs. Jones* was on its way to being published.

If you're wondering what galleys are, it's your typeset book on long, narrow sheets of paper waiting for you to check any errors. I received three sets and was told to give the other two to friends capable of proofreading. Later I was to compare their findings with mine. I couldn't dawdle; all copies had to be mailed back in ten days.

The book was published in paperback and distributed to post exchanges in the United States and overseas. I'll never forget the thrill of seeing my first copy. Eventually, the *Army Times* gave it a favorable review, and CBS News came down to do a radio interview for their "Weekend" show. But the greatest thrill for me was when my cadet son walked into the bookstore at West Point and spied *This Is the Army, Mrs. Jones.*

If you have never been introduced to army life, you may be wondering what the handbook was all about. Thelma and I described what it was like to live on an army post; how to cope with army abbreviations; what to take to Alaska or Hawaii or Germany, etc.; the sequence in rank; how to seat people at a formal dinner party; how to create a gourmet meal in no time; and how to be a successful program chairman. We provided all kinds of recipes and forty different entertainment ideas the new army wives could use when it was their turn to do a program at the club.

But where we helped the most was in the section that interpreted what their husbands would say to them from time to time. Here is an excerpt:

> Suppose your husband comes home for lunch tomorrow and says, "Honey, we had a C&S meeting this morning at the Battle Group CP, and the old man announced that my company is going on a three-day FTX." Would you have any idea as to what he was trying to tell you? Without a doubt, you'd stare at him and wonder what in the world he was talking about. But if you take a look at the following abbreviations and definitions, you'll be able to toss off a few terms of your own the next time he makes such a statement.

The handbook then listed about sixty terms and abbreviations. We also added the Army's unique way of telling time so that Mrs. Jones would know that 2400 ("twenty-four hundred hours") means midnight and that 0600 ("oh-six hundred hours") means 6 a.m.

Using Your Own Experiences

I've gone into some detail about this handbook to show all of you that there may be something in your own experience that can be shared with a number of readers. This informal paperback never became a bestseller, but it stayed in print for seven or eight years, and a copy turned up last year at a flea market nearby. During the past few years, the army has become less demanding in its protocol and club functions, and I hear that many of the wives now hold down jobs in town or even on post. In my day, this kind of freedom was almost unheard of. But I am sure that parts of *This Is the Army, Mrs. Jones* could still help service wives planning to follow their military men all over the world.

Are you in one of the services? Keep a journal or diary and see if you can write an interesting account of your life here or in a foreign country. But realize the fact that that in itself won't sell the book. Your story must fill a need or be so extra-special that many people will buy a copy and tell others about it. Years ago, an army wife in Japan wrote a book called *Over the Bamboo Fence* that sold quite well, but she wrote it when the customs of that country weren't too well known. In 1979, a young graduate of West Point, Lucian Truscott, wrote his first mystery, *Dress Gray*, using his alma mater as the setting. A retired general who lives near here keeps himself busy by writing paperbacks on battles of the Civil War; this area is steeped in history of that period in America's past.

Are you a teacher? Can you write about your experiences in working with your students? Bel Kaufman did that in 1964 when she wrote *Up the Down Staircase*. She used her background as a teacher in a New York City school and fictionalized her story. She added her special touch by building her storyline from administrative memos, student compositions, and interschool communications. Later it was made into a first-rate movie.

Another teacher by the name of Jenny Gray wrote a guidebook for new teachers and called it *The Teacher's Survival Guide, or How to Teach Teen-agers and Live to Tell About It*. She wrote it while living in California, and had it published by Fearon Publishers of Palo Alto. You may wish to look around for a nearby publisher when you do your first book. (You can find some listed in *Writer's Market*.) I don't know Ms. Gray personally, but I do know she went on to write *Teaching Without Tears* a year or two later. She had to be doing something right.

Have you ever heard of William C. Anderson? He's a retired Air Force officer who recently wrote *Home Sweet Home on Wheels*, which tells about the adventures he and his wife experienced traveling in an RV for almost a year. He is also the author of *Hurricane Hunters*, *The Great Bicycle Expedition*, and *When the Offspring Have Sprung*. I should mention that his current book not only relates his travels but also gives advice on motor home and RV living. Have you taken trips during the past few years that would make interesting reading? Think about it. If you're planning a trip around the world, start your journal now. By the time you return, you'll have enough material on hand to fill a book.

Are you into walking these days? Aaron Sussman and Ruth Goode wrote a book about ten years ago and called it *The Magic of Walking*. But they added the extra something by including excerpts on walking by famous men and women in literature. They quote "The Open Road" by Walt Whitman; "The Pleasure of Walking" by Oliver Wendell Holmes; "Departure" by Edna St.

Vincent Millay; "The Pedestrian" by Ray Bradbury; and "The Road Not Taken" by Robert Frost. Find this book at the library; if you have never been thrilled at the thought of going for a walk, you will be when you read this book. If you are already a walker, you may get an idea for a book of your own.

Can your family provide you with material for a book? Begin now to write down some of the things that happened in your childhood. Sam Levenson did, and in his successful book *Everything But Money*, he told about his upbringing in a family of eight brothers and sisters in such a way that he became a popular writer and TV personality. His tales of Jewish life on the Lower East Side of New York will be remembered for a long time. Jean Kerr won recognition when she wrote about her children in *Please Don't Eat the Daisies* and *The Snake Has All the Lines*. If you bemoan the fact that you can't get any writing done around the house because it's so noisy, follow Kerr's example: she usually drove her car down a block or two, parked, and dug out her writing gear. Shirley Jackson, famous for her gothic tales, wrote about her growing family in a book called *My Life Among the Savages;* it's worth reading for its hilarious moments, but also to show you a side to this author's writing that isn't too well known.

Have you ever thought of doing a cookbook? Peg Bracken did, and produced *The I Hate To Cook Book,* filled with 180 quick and easy (and unusual) recipes along with advice about kitchen problems. She slanted her book toward the housewife who felt hostile toward the kitchen. She was amazed at how many women bought her book; they liked her humor—and her tasty dishes. Norma Jean and Carol Darden recently wrote a delightful cookbook, now in paperback, called *Spoon Bread and Strawberry Wine,* which contains the recipes and reminiscences of the sisters' family stretching back to the days before the Civil War.

Several years ago, some senior citizens in Wisconsin who entered the "Yarns of Yesteryear" contest sponsored by the University of Wisconsin Extension Division and the Regional Writers' Association had a great idea. They took nearly a hundred of their glimpses of the past and put them into a book called *We Were Children Then*. It did so well that other compilations are in the offing.

Verna Mae Slone wrote a simple, moving account of her life in the hills and hollows of Kentucky for her grandchildren and called it *What My Heart Wants to Tell*. Her purpose was to dispel the unflattering myth of the "hillbilly," and she traced the hard life of her family as they forced subsistence out of a stubborn and hostile land. Another grandmother named Juretta Murray wrote a book for her grandchildren which told about the wonderful world of astronomy. She called it *Listen, Look, the Stars!* and wrote it in the form of talks to her granddaughters. Her aim in writing the book was to tie the stars to thoughts of God, and to show that friendship with the stars is a fascinating experience. She was able to use her hobby in a different way.

One of the most unusual books I have found while working on this chapter is called *The Storybook Cookbook*. Carol MacGregor had the ingenious idea of selecting twenty-two delicious concoctions mentioned in the classics of children's literature and providing recipes for them. For example, *Misty of Chincoteague* by Marguerite Henry features Chincoteague Pot Pie; *Hans Brinker or The Silver Skates* gives a recipe for waffles; and *Treasure Island* describes how to make chipped beef. The author prefaced each recipe with the paragraph or two that contained the reference to the food, and provided her young readers with step-by-step instructions on preparing it.

The year 1977 will always be an important one to Paula Delfield of Brownsville, Wisconsin: she celebrated her golden wedding anniversary and the birth of her first great-grandchild, and saw her first book come into being. It took her three years of research and writing to finish *The Indian Priest*, a true story of a young man in her town, and she had it accepted after the third try. She is now doing another, and plans to keep on writing books and articles far into the future.

One of the funniest ideas for a book happened to Arue Szura in Castro Valley, California. She burned so many meals that her family—and the local firemen—named her the "The Carbon Queen." When she enrolled in an adult writing class, she decided to make the most of the good-natured kidding going on around her by writing a cookbook. She called it *Where There's Smoke There's Dinner*, and included a number of recipes from the firemen. After being turned down by several publishers, she came to the conclusion that her book didn't appeal to them because it had too much of a local slant. She then took it to a print shop and ordered five hundred copies made. She distributed them to local bookstores and gift shops and sent out mail orders through one of the newspapers. In ten weeks the books were gone. When a revised edition was printed, Arue Szura set up a booth at a carnival in San Francisco where she sold and autographed copies of the new version. She can still remember how embarrassing it was to have fire engines come roaring down her street to put out her kitchen fires, but is pleased that something negative can be turned into something positive.

Query First

Suppose the day comes when you have chosen your idea for a nonfiction book. How should you go about collecting your material? What does an editor look for? How can you convince her that your book will sell? Should you send a query letter or a more detailed book proposal?

Many editors prefer to see a one-page query first. If you choose to go this route, make sure to give the theme or focus of your book in the first paragraph. Follow this with some details on the potential market for your material, and why you believe you are qualified to write this book. You can end your letter with some of your credits, if you have any.

If you receive a favorable response, you can send off a detailed proposal and a more definitive market analysis. You should also include two or three completed chapters and an outline of the rest of your book; actually, the outline is a number of chapter synopses. You will have to name your chapters and do a summary of each one. If you're thinking that all of this adds up to quite a bit of work, you're right. But the editor must be convinced that she is accepting a book that will have sales potential and that she will not lose a great deal of money.

Remember one thing when you query about your book: use a kind of narrative hook, if possible, so the editor will want to keep reading. Your idea will be in competition with many others, and you will have to offer something fresh and different to catch her attention.

If all of this information is just what you've been looking for you may still need some help that's crucial to your book idea. What publishers will be interested in the kind of material you're rounding up? To make sure that the book you have in mind is of the same type published by the house to which you are sending it, take a trip to the library and look for *Literary Market Place*, compiled by Bowker, and thumb through its pages. Here you'll find the addresses of publishers, names of editors, a brief description of the type of book published, and the number of books they do per year. You should also do some browsing in the bookstores to see what is on the market.

Even though you are a beginning writer, it isn't too soon to start a diary or journal to which you can refer later on. I can vouch for the fact that the day will come when you will have enough bits of information to get started on a book. If it happened to me, it can happen to you.

11

Are You on Target
with Your Market?

Nice things have been happening lately to my friend Sam. He's been getting all kinds of checks in the mail along with encouraging words from fiction and nonfiction editors. And I know his secret. He walks around with a copy of the current *Writer's Market* tucked under his arm; it has become his bible, and he knows passages by heart. He is a selling writer because he studies the markets.

Whenever Sam writes a short story or an article, he goes through this directory with an eagle eye, searching for a magazine that his piece is suited to. If the editor insists on a query first, he does his best to compose a letter that will sell his idea. Most of the time, however, he sends off his manuscript with a covering note in which he describes what he is trying to do. He also mentions his qualifications, along with a brief list of credits. He always makes sure that he encloses a SASE.

Market Analysis

As you begin to produce material, you'll find that you have a tendency to latch on to the markets that happen to be on hand. A new one appears in the latest writers' magazine, or one of your friends tells you he's made a sale and why don't you try them, too. But if you're hoping to find a home for your article on raising white orchids, it won't be with your friend's publication that deals with home improvements. If you're sending out fiction, make sure you aren't aiming at a nonfiction market. According to many editors, this happens fairly often.

What's the best way to become familiar with publications? As I've mentioned before, you will be amazed at the number of new magazines and newspapers available. Most of them can be bought at drugstores and supermarkets. Buy some of the ones that appeal to you and read them thoroughly to get the feel of the style used in each one.

If you want to build a library of magazines at home, go to the yard sales and flea markets in your town. Watch for your public library to have a book and magazine sale, where you can pick up a variety of published material for a nominal sum. Exchange magazines with your friends, especially those who belong to writers' clubs. We have been doing that lately in several of my groups, and it has helped tremendously in getting us acquainted with current needs in fiction and nonfiction—and of course we're saving all kinds of money.

But even if you follow through with these suggestions, you must do a bit more. Send for some of the sample magazines and newspapers mentioned in *The Writer* and *Writer's Digest*. Some of them will be free, but others will cost a dollar or two. When you send for them, ask for the free writer's guidelines usually available.

Coping with Rejection

One of the most important tips I have given in this book should be repeated here: Don't send out one manuscript and then sit back and wait for results. If you send out an article or story, it will take time, of course, to do another one. But let an idea take shape as soon as possible and let it grow in your mind a little every day. In the fiction field especially, get under the skin of your characters so that you know them almost as well as you know yourself. In the meantime, protect yourself from a possible rejection of your submission by training yourself to send out a filler or two every week. Later on, you can send out several articles or stories instead, if you wish. But for now, get into the habit of dropping a recipe or a footnote to history into the mail at least once a week.

Once you start writing, you'll find out that rejection slips come in all shapes, sizes, and colors. Some of the messages are terse and read:

> Thank you very much for your recent submission. Unfortunately, it does not suit our current editorial needs.

or

> Thank you for inquiring as to our interest in your project.
> Unfortunately, it does not sound particularly well-suited
> to our list.

But many of them sound like this:

> Thank you for sending your manuscript to be considered for publication.
>
> It has not, however, been selected for publication and is being returned.
>
> We would be happy for the chance to look over your other work which you feel would be suitable for our magazine.

Then there are some that have a personal note written by the editor telling the writer to keep them in mind for other articles or story possibilities. Keep these in a special place on your desk; something in your manuscript caught the fancy of the man or woman in charge.

One of the nicest rejection slips I have ever received read in part:

> Thank you for allowing Children's Press to hold your manuscript, *The Pumpkin People.* The editors were impressed with your work.
>
> We regret that we must return this material. This in no way reflects upon your work. Your writing is excellent, and it is obvious that you have thoroughly researched your subject. After extensive editorial discussion, it was decided to return your material because it is not suited to our present publishing program. Children's Press rarely publishes an individual book. . . .
>
> Thank you again for allowing us to review your work. . . .

One of the most humorous turndowns came from an in-flight magazine, *TWA Ambassador.* I plan to try them again because those editors have a funny bone. They sent a two-part card which read:

> Rejection Slip (Re-jek-shun-slip) n., A verbal crutch used by editors who are too busy and/or lazy to write a personal letter or comment when they refuse to buy a perfectly good manuscript that a smarter editor would snap up in a minute.
>
> That's what a rejection slip is; and that's what this card is. We'd rather write a letter and tell you why we aren't going to

buy your work. But if we did that, with all the manuscripts we receive, we wouldn't have time left to request checks for the few that we do buy.

And you wouldn't like that.

So, don't take this rejection slip personally, and feel free to query again or send more manuscripts. We look at them all. And when we find one that fits exactly what we want, we send another form reply.

A check.

You'll like that even better than a nice letter.

The Editors

Whenever I read this card to my students, they always laugh at its lighthearted approach to one phase of writing that is often unpleasant. But they appreciate my following up with some of the reasons why the editors won't accept the material in front of them. You've already been told some of them, but let's look at a few more:

1. You have exceeded the word limit. It doesn't matter if you tacked on 40 or 50 to a 1,000-word article or story, but if you added 110 to 120, you could be in trouble. If you're more than 10 percent over the limit, this could be a reason for your submission's returning home. Keep in mind that editors have word limits because their space is restricted and they can only use so many pieces.

2. Your material is too trite. If you're doing a story about a typical family complete with dog and cat, add those special touches that make them all a little different from the ones we read about every day. Give them a problem and solution that hasn't been done again and again.

3. Your material is too wordy. There are too many adjectives and adverbs; you've used words that need explanation or should be said more simply.

4. Your story lacks a good plot or theme.

5. Your story sounds contrived in its development.

6. The lead of your article does not grab the reader's attention.

7. Your article needs more facts and research.

8. The magazine has assigned a similar piece to another writer.
9. The magazine has a similar story on hand.
10. The editors believe this subject has been overdone.

When your material comes back, look it over critically, and if you think it still sounds pretty good, mail it out again immediately. In fact, send it to six or seven publications. If it becomes dog-eared in the meantime, retype it. If the day comes when you know you can improve it, analyze what is wrong and revise it.

The rest of this chapter will cover all kinds of markets; some will be for the professional writer, but others will be accessible to the beginner. They cover a range of subjects suitable to men and women from a variety of backgrounds. Read them carefully and see what appeals to you and your interests. Before you take a look at them, I'd like to share the following rejection slip with you. No one knows who the author is, but I tip my hat to him or her for making us chuckle.

A Chinese Editor Rejects a Manuscript

Illustrious brother of the sun and moon: Behold thy servant prostrate before thy feet. I kowtow to thee and beg of thy graciousness thou mayest grant that I may speak and live. Thy honored manuscript has deigned to cast the light of its august countenance upon me. With raptures I have perused it. By the bones of my ancestors, never have I encountered such wit, such pathos, such lofty thoughts. With fear and trembling, I return the writing. Were I to publish the treasure you sent me, the Emperor would order that it should be made the standard, and that none be published except such as equaled it. Knowing literature as I do, and that it would be impossible in ten thousand years to equal what you have done, I send your writing back. Ten thousand times I crave your pardon. Behold, my head is at your feet. Do what you will.

Your servant's servant,
The Editor

Markets for Fillers and Short Humor

Writers who have a flair for creating short and witty items will find a large and lucrative market in magazines and newspapers for their fillers. This is an especially good field for the beginning writer; here he can tell of his personal experiences or elaborate on a favorite joke or come up with light verse, household hints, quips, and recipes. Editors prefer one item to a page, and expect you to give the source of a factual filler or anecdote.

Remember: if you have not heard from the editor in two months or more, redo your carbon and mail it out elsewhere.

The American Legion Magazine, Box 1055, Indianapolis, IN 46206. "Parting Shots" editor needs short, funny anecdotes appealing to military/naval, veterans, older readers; one or two-line gags; humorous verse, to four lines. Pays $15 for anecdotes on acceptance.

Army Magazine, 2425 Wilson Blvd., Arlington, VA 22201. True anecdotes on military subjects. Pays $10 to $35 on publication.

Bicycling, 33 E. Minor Rd., Emmaus, PA 19049. Needs anecdotes and other short items for "Open Road" section, 150 to 200 words. Pays $15 to $25 on publication.

Boys' Life, 1325 Walnut Hill Lane, Irving, TX 75062. Looking for how-to features, to 400 words with photos on hobbies, crafts, science, outdoor skills, etc. Pays from $150.

Chevron USA, P.O. Box 6227, San Jose, CA 95150. Quarterly. True, previously unpublished, humorous anecdotes with a travel tie-in, 200 words. Pays $25 on publication.

Child Life, P.O. Box 567, Indianapolis, IN 46206. Needs puzzles, games, mazes, and rebuses, on health or safety-related subjects, for children seven to nine years. Pays $10 to $15 on publication.

Christian Life, 396 E. St. Charles Rd., Wheaton, IL 60188. News items, to 200 words, on trends, ideas, unique personalities and ministries, and events of interest to Christians. Also looking for short pieces, 500 to 800 words, of interest to women: recipes, handicrafts, true adventures. Pays $5 to $25.

Down East, Camden, ME 04843. Anecdotes about Maine, to 1,000 words, for "I Remember." Humorous anecdotes, to 300 words, for "It Happened Down East." Pays $10 to $50 on acceptance.

Expecting, 686 Third Avenue, New York, NY 10017. Looking for anecdotes about pregnancy for "Happenings." Pays $10 on publication.

Farm Woman News, P.O. Box 643, Milwaukee, WI 53201. Short verse, 20 to 25 lines, and fillers, to 250 words, on the rural experience. Pays from $40 on publication.

Fate, 500 Hyacinth Pl., Highland Park, IL 60035. Factual fillers, to 300 words, on strange or psychic or mystic personal experiences. Pays $1 to $10.

Field and Stream, 1515 Broadway, New York, NY 10036. Fillers on hunting, camping, fishing, etc., 500 to 1,000 words, for "How It's Done," and "Did you Know?" cartoons. Pays $250 to $350, and $100 for cartoons on acceptance.

Games, 515 Madison Avenue, New York, NY 10022. Puzzles, word and number games, riddles, codes, mazes, trivia, and other games. Pays varying rates.

Golf Digest, 495 Westport Avenue, Norwalk, CT 06856. Short fact items, anecdotes, quips, jokes, light verse related to golf. True humorous or odd incidents, to 200 words. Pays from $25 on acceptance.

Good Housekeeping, 959 Eighth Avenue, New York, NY 10019. Light verse and very short humorous prose. Pays from $10 to $100.

Grit, 208 Third Street, Williamsport, PA 17701. Brief anecdotal features, from 30 words, on interesting, amusing, heartwarming, and inspiring subjects. Humorous verse. Pays 12¢ a word for prose, $6 for four lines of verse.

Guideposts, 747 Third Avenue, New York, NY 10017. Inspirational anecdotes, to 250 words. Pays $10 to $50 on acceptance.

Home Life, 127 Ninth Avenue N., Nashville, TN 37234. Southern Baptist. Personal-experience pieces, 100 to 500 words, on Christian marriage and family relationships. Pays 4¢ a word, on acceptance.

Inflight, P.O. Box 10019, Ogden, UT 84409. Humor, for male, business-oriented audience. Pays 15¢ a word on acceptance. Query.

Ladies' Home Journal, Three Park Avenue, New York, NY 10016. Brief anecdotes and poems about the funny business of being a woman today for "Last Laughs" section. Pays $25.

Mature Years, 201 Eighth Avenue S., Nashville, TN 37202. Poems, cartoons, puzzles, jokes, anecdotes, to 300 words, for older adults. Pays 4¢ a word on acceptance.

Modern Romances, 215 Lexington Avenue, New York, NY 10016. Short items, to 300 words, for "Little Things That Say I Love You" and "Our Family Tradition." Pays $25 thirty days after month of publication.

Organic Gardening, 33 E. Minor Street, Emmaus, PA 18049. Fillers, 100 to 500 words, on gardening experiences; how-to's, solutions of problems, etc. Photos of lawn art. Cartoons, cartoon ideas. Gardening riddles. Horticultural "bloopers" in local papers, etc. Pays $25 to $200 on publication.

Parents, 685 Third Avenue, New York, NY 10017. Short items on solutions of child care-related problems for "Parents Exchange." Pays $20 on publication.

Playboy, 919 N. Michigan Avenue, Chicago, IL 60611. Address Party Jokes Editor or After Hours Editor. Jokes, short original material on new trends, lifestyles, personalities, humorous news items. Pays $50 for jokes, on acceptance; $50 to $350 for "After Hours" items on publication.

Popular Mechanics, 224 W. 57th Street, New York, NY 10019. How-to pieces, from 300 words, with photos and sketches, on home improvement and shop and craft projects. Pays $25 to $100 on acceptance.

Reader's Digest, Pleasantville, NY 10570. Anecdotes for "Life in These United States," "Humor in Uniform," "Campus Comedy," and "All in a Day's Work." Pays $300 on publication. Also looking for short items for "Toward More Picturesque Speech." Pays $50.

The Saturday Evening Post, 1100 Waterway Blvd., Indianapolis, IN 46202. Humor and satire, to 500 words; jokes for "Post Scripts." Pays $15 on publication.

Skiing Magazine, One Park Avenue, New York, NY 10016. Items to 600 words, on skiing; humorous vignettes, fillers on skiing oddities. Pays from 15¢ a word on acceptance.

Sunday Digest, 850 N. Grove Avenue, Elgin, IL 60120. Inspirational anecdotes, short humor (500 words). Writers' guidelines on request. Pays 7¢ to 10¢ a word on acceptance.

Travel Smart, Dobbs Ferry, NY 10522. Interesting, unusual, or helpful travel-related tips, to 250 words. Pays $5 to $15 on publication. Query.

Winning, 15115 S. 76 E. Avenue, Bixby, OK 74008. Short pieces, 400 to 600 words, on winning contests, sweepstakes, lotteries, games shows, bingo, Vegas-style gambling, etc. Pays 5¢ a word on publication.

Volkswagen's World, Volkswagen of America, Troy, MI 48099. Anecdotes, to 100 words, about Volkswagen owners' experiences; cartoons, humorous photos of Volkswagens. Pays from $15 on acceptance.

Woman's Day, 1515 Broadway, New York, NY 10036. Short items on personal instructive family experiences and tips for "Neighbors"; practical suggestions for homemakers. Pays $50 on publication.

Women's Sports and Fitness, 310 Town and Country Village, Palo
   Alto, CA 94301. Short pieces, on nutrition, beauty, health, and
   new products for the active woman; short profiles of up-and-com-
   ing female athletes or other female sports figures; book reviews;
   opinion pieces. Pays from $25 on publication.

The Article Market

Editors in the article category are looking for how-to pieces on
health, hobbies, and sports; features on people, places, events,
trends, and new ideas. They are also interested in personal experience stories and humor. Beginners have a good chance of hitting this
market if they keep in mind that an article needs quotes by experts in
the field, an anecdote or two, and some pertinent examples. You
should also keep in mind that regional magazines and newspapers
are receptive to this kind of writing. You should check into some of
the literary and "little" magazines; even though most of them pay in
copies, you'll get that byline you've been hoping for. The following
markets have been carefully chosen so that every kind of beginning
writer can find a magazine or newspaper leaning toward his or her
interests.

The American Legion Magazine, Box 1055, Indianapolis, IN 46206.
   Looking for war remembrance pieces, topics of contemporary interest, and little-known happenings in American history. Length
   not more than 2,000 words. Also interested in 750-word commen-
   taries on contemporary problems and points of view. Query first.

American Baby Magazine, 575 Lexington Avenue, New York, NY
   10022. Most readers are first-time parents. Book excerpts, how-to
   (some aspect of pregnancy or child care); interviews with experts
   in maternal/infant health or child-care; and personal experience
   (should give advice to new parents or parents to be). Length: 500-
   2,000 words. Pays $100-$400. Query or send complete manuscript. Send brief biography with submissions.

Americana, 29 W. 38th Street, New York, NY 10018. General interest
   (crafts, architecture, cooking, gardening, restorations, antiques,
   preservation, decorating, collecting, people who are active in

these fields and museums); and travel (to historic sites, restored villages, hotels, inns, and events celebrating the past). Length: 2,000 words minimum. Query. Send for writer's guidelines with a SASE. Pays $400 minimum.

Cats Magazine, Box 10766, Southport, NC 28461. Cat health, cat breed articles, articles on the cat in art, literature, history, human culture, cats in the news. Cat pets of personalities. Could use an occasional humorous article portraying cats and humans. Length: 800-2,500 words. Pays $15-$75 and extra for photos. Free sample copy.

Christian Home, Box 189, 1908 Grand Avenue, Nashville, TN 37202. Articles on parenting, marriage, and devotional life, 1,000 to 1,500 words, for couples and families. Pays about 6¢ a word, on acceptance. Free sample copy and guidelines.

The Christian Science Monitor, One Norway Street, Boston, MA 02115. Articles on lifestyle trends, women's rights, family, parenting, consumerism, fashion, and food; interviews; literary essays, to 800 words, for "Home Forum." Pays varying rates, on acceptance.

Dynamic Years, 215 Long Beach Boulevard, Long Beach, CA 90802. Articles, 1,000 to 2,500 words, on preretirement planning, career changes, sideline businesses, personal adjustments, financial and legal problems, and crafts, for working Americans in their middle years. Profiles, humor. Free sample copy and guidelines.

Europe for Travelers!, Europe Incorporated, 408 Main Street, Nashua, NH 03060. Quarterly magazine on Europe for traveling Americans. Mostly destination pieces. Also how-to (open to proposals); light humor (but not satire or sarcasm); and personal experience. No religious, political, or complaint-type articles. Query or send complete manuscript. Any length up to 2,000 words. Pays $10-$100. Writer's guidelines available with a SASE.

Family Weekly, 1515 Broadway, New York, NY 10036. Short, lively articles on prominent individuals, health, medicine, money management, and family advice. Pays from $200, on acceptance. Query.

Ford Times, Room 765, P.O. Box 1899, Dearborn, MI 48121-1899. Articles, to 1,500 words, on contemporary life and trends, travel, outdoor activities. Profiles of personalities, well-known or not. Pays to $750, on acceptance. Query. Free sample copy and guidelines.

Games, 515 Madison Avenue, New York, NY 10022. Short articles on unusual games and original games and puzzles. Pays varying rates, on publication. Query.

Gentlemen's Quarterly, 350 Madison Avenue, New York, NY 10017. Articles, 1,500 to 4,000 words, on politics, lifestyles, trends, grooming, nutrition, sports, travel, money, and business; profiles. Query with clips. Pays $750 to $3,000, on acceptance. (Try to obtain copy of magazine from editor, if possible.)

Guideposts, 747 Third Avenue, New York, NY 10017. True first-person accounts, 250 to 1,500 words, stressing how faith in God helps people cope with life. Anecdotal fillers, to 250 words. Pays $100 to $400, $10 to $25 for fillers, on acceptance.

Grit, 208 W. Third Street, Williamsport, PA 17701. Articles, to 500 words, on religion, communities, jobs, recreation, families, and coping. Pays 12¢ a word, on acceptance. (Look for it at your supermarket).

Inflight, Meridian Publishing Company, Inc. Box 10010, Ogden, UT 84409. A bimonthly magazine distributed by business and professional firms, particularly commercial airlines. General interest, historic/nostalgic; humor, interview/profile; photo feature; sports. Query. Length: 1,000-2,000 words. Pay 15¢ a word. Sample copy for $1 and 9x12 SASE. Writer's guidelines available.

McCall's, 230 Park Avenue, New York, NY 10169. Interesting, unusual and topical first-person essays, narratives, reports on health, home management, social trends relating to women of all ages, 1,000 to 3,000 words. Humor. Human interest stories. Essays 1,000 words, for "Back Talk," a forum for airing fresh and often controversial views on all subjects. Pays top rates, on acceptance. Query for articles.

The Mother Earth News, Box 70, Hendersonville, NC 28791. Emphasizes "back-to-basics, how-to for individuals who seek a more self-directed way of life." Looking for articles on home business, how-to, low-cost housing, seasonal cooking, gardening, and crafts. Sample copy $3, writer's guidelines for SASE and 39¢ postage. Length: 300-3,000 words. Pays $100/published page minimum.

The Retired Officer Magazine, 201 N. Washington Street, Alexandria, VA 22314. Recent military history, humor, hobbies, travel, second-career opportunities, and current affairs. Also upbeat articles on aging, human interest, and features pertinent to a retired officer milieu. True military experiences are also useful. Length: 1,000-2,500 words. Pays $100-$400. Free sample copy and writer's guidelines.

Silver Circle, 4900 Rivergrade Road, Irwindale, CA 91706. Looking for general interest articles and features for older audiences, 50 and up. Needs book excerpts, historical/nostalgic, how-to, humor/interview/profile, personal experience, photo feature, travel, and financial articles. (This magazine is published by a savings and loan company; they don't want any material on investing). Length: 500-4,000 words. Pays $75-$600. Query. Sample copy available.

Woman's Day, 1515 Broadway, New York, NY 10036. This magazine is very receptive to freelancers. Pieces should run 1,000 to 2,500 words and should have a human-interest or self-help slant; popular topics include careers, relationships, consumer tips, psychology, and family care. Also uses insightful opinion essays, 900 to 1,200 words, for "Reflections" column. Pays top rates.

Woodmen of the World Magazine, 1700 Farnam Street, Omaha, NE 68102. General interest articles which appeal to the American family, travel, history, art, new products, how-to, sports, hobbies, food, home decorating, humor, and think pieces. Length: 2,000 words or less. Pays 5¢ a word. Free sample copy available.

Working Mother, 230 Park Avenue, New York, NY 10169. Looking for well-developed articles geared to a readership of women who are "juggling jobs and families." Length: 1,500 to 2,500 words. Payment varies from $500 to $800. Query. Sample copy available for $2.50 and 8½x12 SASE. Writer's guidelines for SASE.

The Juvenile Market

Freelancers, beginners and professionals alike, will find this market a receptive one. Editors are looking for all types of fiction and nonfiction along with humor and poetry slanted toward children and teenagers.

Included in this list of general publications are some of the religious magazines. These editors want material that promotes character-building without preaching. A beginner has a good chance here if he sends for a sample copy and follows the guidelines.

Children's Digest, Children's Better Health Institute, Box 567, Indianapolis, IN 46206. Magazine published eight times a year covering children's health for children eight-ten. Pays on publication. Historical, interview/profile, craft ideas, health, nutrition, hygiene, exercise and safety. Length: 500-1,200 words. Pays 6¢ a word. No queries. Sample copy for 75¢; writer's guidelines for SASE.

Cobblestone, Cobblestone Publishing, Inc., 20 Grove Street, Peterborough, NH 03458. Monthly magazine covering history (American) for children ages eight-fourteen. Each issue presents a theme. All material must relate to that month's theme. Looking for historical/nostalgic, how-to, interview, and personal experience. Fiction should cover stories of adventure, history, humor, and biography. Sample copy $2.95. Guidelines available for SASE. Pays up to 15¢ a word.

Crusader Magazine, Box 7244, Grand Rapids, MI 49510. This publication shows boys (nine-fourteen) how God is at work in their lives and the world around them. Looking for articles on sports, outdoor activities, bike riding, science, crafts, etc., and problems. Length: 500-1,500 words. Also looking for fiction appealing to a boy's sense of adventure or sense of humor. Length: 750-1,500 words. Pays 3¢ a word. Writer's guidelines availble for SASE.

Digit Magazine, The Video/Computing Connection for Young People, Beckwith/Benton Communications, Inc., 2342 North Point, San Francisco, CA 94123. Bimonthly magazine covering computers/high technology for use as a classroom tool. Written for the ten-sixteen age group. Needs articles dealing with technology, new products, profiles, and humor, all appealing to young people. Length: 1,000-2,500 words. Pays $50-$500. Sample copy $3; guidelines for SASE.

Happy Times, Eagle Systems International, 5600 N. University Avenue, Provo, UT 86404. Published ten times a year for children ages three-six with emphasis on educational and moral content. Looking for articles on how-to, travel, history/nostalgia, and unique puzzles that instruct children. Length: 50-300 words. Writers must see publication before submitting. Sample copy available for five first class stamps. Free guidelines for SASE. (Pays $10-$50.)

Highlights for Children, 803 Church Street, Honesdale, PA 18431. Magazine for children ages two-twelve. Interested in articles on history, science, life in other countries, sports, and other factual features. These must be written by persons with mastery in their fields. Contributions, however, are always welcomed from new writers. Length: 900 words maximum. Pays $65 minimum. Also looking for fiction stories which will appeal to boys and girls. They should be vivid and full of action. Length: 400-900 words. Pays $65 minimum. Sample copy of magazine $2.25. Free writer's guidelines for SASE.

Nautica, The Magazine of the Sea for Young People, Spinnaker Press, Inc., Pickering Wharf, Salem, MA 01970. This publication covers all aspects of the nautical and water world. Written for children ages eight-fourteen. Needs articles on history, personal experience, how-to, and photo features. Length: 1,000-1,800 words. Pays 10¢-25¢ a word. Sample copy $1.25. Free writer's guidelines for SASE (9x12).

Pennywhistle Press, Gannett Co., Inc., Box 500-P, Washington, D.C. 20044. A weekly tabloid supplement with stories and features for children ages six-twelve. Wants general-interest articles, sports and crafts, and photo features. Length: 500 words maximum. Pays $50 maximum. Also needs fiction. Length: 250-850 words. Pays variable rate. Could use short poems (traditional). Sample copy for 50¢, SASE. Writer's guidelines for SASE.

R-A-D-A-R, 8121 Hamilton Avenue, Cincinnati, OH 45231. Weekly for children in grades three-six in Christian Sunday schools. Needs articles on hobbies and handicrafts, nature, famous people, seasonal subjects, etc., written from a Christian viewpoint. Length: 500-1,000 words. Pays 2¢ a word. Also looking for short stories of heroism, adventure, travel, mystery, animals, and biography. Writers who want to write for them should send for a theme list. Fiction length: up to 1,000 words. Pays 2¢ a word maximum. Free sample copy.

Young American, Student News, Young American Publishing Co., Inc., Box 12409, Portland, OR 97212. A monthly 16-24-page tabloid inserted in nine suburban newspapers for students ages four-sixteen. Subjects vary from world politics to children making headlines, and material is easy to digest as well as timely and pertinent. In nonfiction, looking for expose (pertaining to children); how-to make money for kids, (150 words); interview/profile; and technical (science). Length: 150-300 words. Pays 7¢ a word. In fiction, looking for stories of fantasy, humor, mystery, science fiction, and western. Also Christmas stories, 700-900 words. Pays 7¢ a word. Sample copy for SASE (37¢ postage). Free guidelines with SASE.

The Fiction Market

Beginners as well as experienced writers have a chance to sell short-shorts in this field. They can try to do a mystery, a love story, an adventure, a gothic, or an old-fashioned western. Editors warn, however, that the competition is keen, and that the novice should become familiar with the magazine he or she is aiming for. They also suggest it would be worthwhile to try the special-interest and regional magazines and even a literary publication that pays in copies. They can be stepping-stones to bigger and better things later on.

Alfred Hitchcock's Mystery Magazine, Davis Publications, Inc., 380 Lexington Avenue, New York, NY 10017. Well-plotted mystery, suspense, and crime fiction, 1,000 to 14,000 words. Submissions by new writers strongly encouraged. Writer's guidelines for SASE.

Analog: Science Fiction and Science Fact, 380 Lexington Avenue, New York, NY 10017. Science fiction, with human characters in believable future or alien settings: short stories, 3,000-7,500 words; novelettes, 10,000-20,000 words; serials, to 70,000 words. Pays to 6¢ a word, on acceptance. Sample copy $2.50 (no SASE needed). Writer's guidelines for SASE.

Boys' Life, 1325 Walnut Hill Lane, Irving, TX 75062. Publication of Boy Scouts of America. Fiction, 1,000-3,200 words, for eight-eighteen-year-old boys. Pays from $350, on acceptance.

Capper's Weekly, 616 Jefferson Avenue, Topeka, KS 66607. Novel-length mysteries and romance stories; no short stories. Pays $150-$200. Query. Sample copy 55¢.

Cat Fancy, Fancy Publications, Inc., Box 6050, Mission Viejo, CA 92690. Needs stories of adventure, fantasy, history, and humor. Nothing written with cats speaking. Length: 500-3,000 words. Pays 3¢ a word. Also needs all kinds of poems pertaining to cats. Sample copy $3. Free guidelines for SASE.

Chesapeake Bay Magazine, 1819 Bay Ridge Avenue, MD 21403. Short stories, to 12 pages; must be related to Chesapeake Bay area. Pays $75-$85, on acceptance. Sample copy $2; guidelines available.

Dog Fancy, Fancy Publications, Inc., Box 6050, Mission Viejo, CA

92690. They need stories of adventure, fantasy, history, and humor. Length: 500-3,000 words. Pays 3¢ a word. Sample copy $3. Guidelines available for SASE. (Need freelancers who write with feeling and sensitivity).

Ellery Queen's Mystery Magazine, 380 Lexington Avenue, New York, NY 10017. High-quality detective, crime, and mystery stories, 4,000-6,000 words. "First Stories" by unpublished writers. Pays 3¢ to 8¢ a word.

Family Circle, 488 Madison Avenue, New York, NY 10022. Family-oriented fiction, to 2,500 words, for women, short stories with interesting, romantic, fanciful, or philosophical viewpoints; animal stories, short shorts, two pages. Pays from $500, on acceptance.

Farm Woman News, P.O. Box 643, Milwaukee, WI 53201. Interested in stories of adventure, mainstream, suspense, western, and humor. Length: 1,000-1,500 words. Pays $75-$200. Sample copy $2.50; free writer's guidelines for SASE.

Golf Digest, 495 Westport Avenue, Norwalk, CT 06856. Unusual or humorous stories, to 2,000 words, about golf; golf "fables," to 1,000 words. Pays 20¢ a word, on acceptance.

Good Housekeeping, 959 Eighth Avenue, New York, NY 10019. Short stories, 2,000 to 5,000 words, with strong identification figures for women, by published writers and "beginners with demonstrable talent." Novel condensations or excerpts. Pays top rates.

Isaac Asimov's Science Fiction Magazine, 380 Lexington Avenue, New York, NY 10017. Short science fiction and fantasies, to 15,000 words. Pays 5¢ to 7¢ a word, on acceptance. Writer's guidelines available for SASE.

Ladycom, 1732 Wisconsin Avenue, Washington, DC 20007. Fiction, dealing with slice-of-life, romance, and suspense. Military family life or relationship themes only. Query. Length: 1,500-2,500 words. Pays $200-$250. Sample copy $1. Free writer's guidelines.

Mature Living, 127 Ninth Avenue, Nashville, TN 37234. Looking for stories covering everyday living, humor, and religious. This is a Christian publication for retired senior adults 60 + . Length: 925-1,500 words. Pays 4¢ a word. Free sample copy and guidelines.

Published!, Platen Publishing Company, 14240 Bledsoe Street, Sylmar, CA 91342. This is a fairly new publication which encourages fledgling writers as well as those established in the writing trade. Looking for short stories, 900-1,800 words. Pays 5¢ a word. Free sample copy; guidelines for a #10 SASE (first class).

Redbook, 224 W. 57th Street, New York, NY 10019. Needs fresh, distinctive short stories, of interest to women, about love and love relationships, being a parent or dealing with one, friendship, careers, or confronting basic contemporary issues. Length: 1,400-5,000 words. Pays $850 to $1,000. Free guidelines available for SASE.

Running Times, Inc., Suite 20, 144145 Jefferson Davis Highway, Woodbridge, VA 22191. Emphasizes running, jogging, holistic health, and fitness. Looking for stories of adventure, fantasy, and humor. Subjects must involve runners or running. Length: 700-2,500 words. Pays $50-$200. Sample copy $2.

The Saturday Evening Post, 1100 Waterway Boulevard, Indianapolis, IN 46202. Fiction needs: adventure, fantasy, humor, mainstream, mystery, romance, science fiction, suspense, and western. Query. Length: 1,000-5,000 words. Pays $150-$750. Free guidelines for SASE.

Sports Afield, 250 W. 55th Street, New York, NY 10019. Fiction, on hunting and fishing, and related topics. Outdoor adventure stories; humor. Pays top rates, on acceptance.

Sunshine Magazine, Litchfield, IL 62056. Wholesome fiction, 900 to 1,200 words; short stories for youth, 400 to 700 words. Pays to $100, on acceptance. Sample copy for 50¢; writer's guidelines for SASE.

'Teen, 8490 Sunset Boulevard, Los Angeles, CA 90069. Short stories, 2,500 to 4,000 words: mystery, travel, adventure, romance, humor for teens. Pays from $100, on acceptance. This publication is for teenage girls.

Torch Romances, P.O. Box 3307, McLean, VA 22103. Romantic suspense short stories, 12,000 words, with sensual love scenes; avoid plots that contain murder, drugs, and excess violence. Pays flat rate or royalty. Tip sheet for SASE.

Woman's World, P.O. Box 6700, Englewood, NJ 07631. Fast-moving short stories, about 4,500 words, with light romantic theme. Mini-mysteries, 1,500 words, with "whodunit" or "howdunit" theme. No science fiction, fantasy, or historical romance. Pays $1,000 for short stories, $500 mini-mysteries, on acceptance. Sample copy $1 and self-addressed mailing label. Writer's guidelines for SASE.

Working Mother, 230 Park Avenue, New York, NY. Realistic short stories that are relevant to working mothers' lives. Length: 2,000 words (average). Pays about $500 for a story. Sample copy $1.95; writer's guidelines for SASE.

Yankee, Dublin, NH 03444. High-quality, literary short fiction, to 3,500 words, with setting in or compatible with New England. Emphasis is on character development. Pays $750. Free sample copy and guidelines.

The Book Market

Many hardcover and paperback publishing houses are looking for talented new authors and are reading "over the transom" submissions. Make sure you send them a query first. If you are doing a novel, describe the main characters, plot, and setting. If you are doing a nonfiction book, send an outline. Do not send your completed manuscript until you hear from the publisher in response to your query.

Acropolis Books, LTD., 2400 17th Street, NW Washington, D.C. 20009. Interested in nonfiction: how-to, reference, and self-help.

Subjects include health, beauty/fashion, and money management. Also looking for books on early childhood. Free book catalogue.

Arco Publishing, Inc., 215 Park Avenue, New York, NY 10003. Nonfiction needs: needle crafts, pet care and training, horses (all aspects); project-oriented science (young adult); how-to; and militaria. Prefers letter of inquiry with a contents page and one sample chapter.

Avalon Books, Thomas Bouregy & Co., Inc., 401 Lafayette Street, New York, NY 10003. Looking for well-plotted, fast-moving, light romances, romance-mysteries, gothics, westerns, and nurse-romance books of about 50,000 words. Submit one-page synopsis or complete manuscript. Pays $400 advance.

Bradbury Press, 866 3rd Avenue, New York, NY 10011. Publishes hardcover originals for children and young adults. Fiction needs: picture books, contemporary fiction, adventure, and humor. No fantasy or religious material. Book catalogue for SASE and 88¢ postage. Offers $3,000 advance royalty.

Dodd, Mead and Co., 79 Madison Avenue, New York, NY 10016. Publishes book-length manuscripts. Length: 70,000-100,000 words average. Looking for high quality: mysteries, and romantic novels of suspense, biography, popular science, travel, sports, and music. Write for permission before sending manuscript. E.P. Dutton, 2 Park Avenue, New York, NY 10016. Publisher of children's books. Looking for picture books; Smart Cats (beginning readers); stories for ages eight-twelve; Skinny Books (Hi-lo for ages twelve and up). Send query letter first on all except picture books. Offers variable advance.

Houghton Mifflin Co., 2 Park Street, Boston, MA 12108. Publishes hardcover and paperback originals and paperback reprints. In nonfiction: needs Americana, natural history, animals, biography, cookbooks, health, history, how-to, politics, psychology, and self-help. Query. In fiction: historical, mainstream, mystery, science fiction, and suspense. Query.

Alfred A. Knopf, Inc., 201 E. 50th Street, New York, NY 10022. Publishes hardcover and paperback originals and paperback reprints. Looking for book-length nonfiction, including books of scholarly merit. Preferred length: 40,000-150,000 words. Query. Also looking for book-length fiction from known or unknown writers. Length: 30,000-150,000 words. Submit complete manuscript.

Prentice-Hall, Inc., Business and Professional Books Division, Gulf + Western, Inc., Sylvan Avenue, Englewood Cliffs, N.J. 07632. Interested only in nonfiction. Needs how-to, reference, self-help, and technical. Subjects include business and economics, recreation, sports, real estate, law, accounting, computers, and education. Query or submit outline/synopsis and sample chapters. Free book catalogue and guidelines.

Charles Scribner's Sons, 115 5th Avenue, New York, NY 10003. Some 20 percent of their books are from first-time authors. Publishes adult general fiction and nonfiction, practical books, science for the layman, and health and business books. Queries only. Free manuscript guidelines.

Sierra Club Books, 2034 Fillmore Street, San Francisco, CA 94115. Publishes hardcover and paperback originals and reprints. Nonfiction: Animals, health, natural history, how-to (outdoors), juveniles, nature, philosophy, photography, recreation (outdoors), science, sports, and travel. Query. Fiction: Adventure, historical, mainstream, and science fiction. Query. Free book catalogue.

Silhouette Books, 300 E. 42nd Street, New York, NY 10017. Publishes mass market paperback originals. About 10 percent of books from first-time authors. Interested in romance (contemporary stories for adults and young adults). Pays royalty. Send query letter, two-page synopsis, and SASE to head of line. Manuscript guidelines for SASE.

Tempo Books, 200 Madison Avenue, New York, NY 10016. Publishes hardcover reprints and paperback originals. Needs contemporary romances and problem novels for ages ten to fourteen. Submit outline/synopsis and sample chapters. Guidelines for SASE.

Ten Speed Press, Box 7123, Berkeley, CA 94707. Publishes trade paperback originals and reprints. About 5 percent of books are from first-time authors. Offers average $3,000 advance. Interested in books on Americana, gardening, careers, cookbooks, business, cooking and foods, humor, law, self-help, hobbies, recreation, and travel. Submit outline and sample chapters. Free book catalogue.

Tyndale House Publishers, Inc., 336 Gundersen Drive, Wheaton, IL 60187. Publishes hardcover and trade paperback originals and hardcover and mass paperback reprints. About 25 percent of books from first-time authors. Nonfiction: Religious books only; personal experience, family living, marriage, inspirational, Bible prophecy, theology and doctrine, and church history. Fiction: Christian romance, western, and adventure. Free book catalogue and writer's guidelines.

Zebra Books, 475 Park Avenue, New York, NY 10016. About 60 percent of books from first-time authors. Publishes mass market paperback originals and reprints. Nonfiction: Biography, how-to, humor, and self-help. Subjects include health, history, and psychology. They are open to many areas, including self-help, stress, money management, child-rearing, health, war (WW II and Vietnam), and celebrity biographies. Fiction: Adventure, confession, erotica, gothic, historical, horror, humor, mainstream, romance and suspense. Tip sheet available. Book catalogue for business size SASE and 39¢ postage.

12

Do Not Fold, Staple, or Mutilate: Preparing and Sending Out Your Manuscript

One of the greatest moments in your life as a new writer will take place on the day you send your creative offspring into the big wide world of publishing. But before you do that, give it a fighting chance to make a good impression no matter where it goes. You can help immensely by making sure you have done all you can before it sets off on its journey.

Do you talk to your typewriter? This really isn't a strange question; I'm sure you talk to your car. For many years to come, this machine will be your constant companion, your bosom buddy, your alter ego, your Lorelei beckoning you to write, and your right-hand man.

Typing Tips

The typewriter should head the list of requirements for making a manuscript look professional. No editor will ever accept material done in longhand. If you don't have a typewriter, pick up a secondhand one as soon as possible and teach yourself touch typing. There are books for home study, but courses are now available in adult education programs throughout the country. You may prefer a manual to an electric; I used a Royal portable manual for many years and it did become my friend. I now own a small electric Royal that seems to do my thinking for me on days when my mind is out to lunch; there are times when I marvel at what is typed on the page in front of me. (This typewriter cost only $99 at a sale seven years ago; the model is no longer around.) Do some checking before you do any buying, and watch for special sales. Put up an ad in the library or at the supermarket; you may find someone getting ready to unload his machine for a nominal price. If you are already planning to buy a brand-new one, study the variety of brand names, and ask for a service agreement in writing.

In the meantime, you can get your typing done by a friend or someone who advertises in your local newspaper. You can also find a typist via ads in *The Writer* and *Writer's Digest*, which give details on the price, the kind of typewriter, and his or her qualifications. If you use this service, your material must be mailed flat with a thin piece of cardboard to keep it from bending, plus a large brown envelope that is self-addressed and stamped. You want to make sure that when it is returned, it will not be tattered and torn.

Paper Pointers

What about the kind of paper you use? When you are ready for your final draft, make sure your paper is white and measures 8½x11. The story is told that Jacqueline Susann used pink and blue and yellow for her rough drafts when she was writing her novels, but the final one was always white. You'll find many brands of paper to choose from, but one of the best and not too expensive is labeled 25 percent cotton fiber content. Also look for the sign that says "20-pound bond"; this kind has a touch of quality about it, and seems to hold up better than the others.

If you are not the world's best typist, you may already be using erasable paper, which can be a boon to writers who face the typewriter with trepidation. The next time you replenish your supply, look for the corrasable bond now on the market. It costs a little more, but it will not smear as easily. One word of caution: Some editors will not accept manuscripts on this kind of paper. Test it yourself: rub some of your rough-draft pages together and see if it smears. This is the reason why it's frowned upon.

When you are typing your material, be sure to make a carbon copy. Every now and then, a manuscript gets lost, and this will be the only way you can redo your hard work. Buy a medium-weight brand if you can, or invest in cheaper grade mimeo paper that comes in pastel shades and is called "second sheets." It's a good idea to jot down on these carbons the name of your manuscript, the date it was mailed out, and to whom.

Editors are also not too thrilled by articles and stories that are hard to read because they have been done in unusual typewritten characters. They prefer pica or elite any day over script, italics, all capitals, old English, and the like. From what I have gathered, your best bet is the pica with ten characters to the inch or the elite with twelve.

The Final Draft

Let's suppose the time has come for you to do your final draft. Pay close attention to page 1; it will separate you from the know-nothings. First of all, don't use any kind of cover sheet. Editors want to see that top page immediately. In the upper left corner type your name and address, including zip code, on three single-spaced lines. Then move over to the extreme right and type the approximate number of words, using an abbreviation, if you wish, so that it reads Appr. 850 words. If you are worried about the rights you are selling, mention them in single lines under the wordage. (More details on rights will be discussed later on.)

Without a doubt you'll have a merry time when you sit down and count the words of your manuscript. Even if you are a brilliant mathematician, you'll come up with a different tally every time you do it. One way is to count the exact number of words on the first three pages of your manuscript (running up to twenty-five pages), divide the total by three and multiply the result by the number of pages. If you're shaking your head right now, let's take an example. Your manuscript runs ten pages with the first page containing 190 words; the second has 304; and the third has 294. They add up to 788. Divide by three and that comes to 263. Multiply by ten, and your total number of words will be 2,630. Another way is to estimate to the nearest round number by multiplying the average number of words in a line by the average number of lines on a page, and then multiplying that number by the number of the manuscript pages. I think, however, that you should keep in mind that the average double-spaced page usually runs about 250 words. This is a gauge that many writers use when they are typing, and one that my students are grateful for.

Let's get back to that first page once more. If you reread Chapter 4, on fillers, you will see how it should look, but it bears repeating. About one-third down the page, the title is typed in capital letters (make sure it's centered) with the word "by" beneath it (centered), and your name or pen name under that. Each item, by the way, should be double-spaced. Some writers do their titles in upper- and lowercase instead of capitals; I doubt if there is a cardinal rule that it must be one way or the other. But I have learned that the first page is never numbered.

Moving right along, after typing your title and byline, drop down three double spaces, indent five letterspaces, and begin your article or story. All of your paragraphs should be indented five spaces throughout your material. Margins should be 1¼ inches on all sides of each page except, of course, for page 1. And remember, all of your work must be double-spaced.

Your other pages should be numbered in the upper right-hand corner. Your surname or a key word from your title should appear in the upper left; if a page or two should stray from the whole manuscript, it will be a simple matter to identify it. When you get to the end of your manuscript, drop down about three double spaces and type "The End." Center it so that it presents a neat appearance.

I mentioned before that you can specify rights on that first page, but some editors may think it a bit presumptuous on your part as a beginning writer to make that statement. It might be wise to wait until you have picked up some credits—and you will. But you should become familiar with some of the terms used in this business of writing and selling, and here are a few definitions:

First North American serial rights means that a magazine is buying the exclusive right to publish the material for the first time and only once.

Second serial rights gives the magazine the right to reprint the material once after its original publication.

All periodical rights means that the magazine is buying the exclusive right to print and reprint the material here and in foreign countries.

Someday, when you have sold a book, you will have to sign a contract, which will tell you in detail the rights the publisher is buying and the ones that belong to you.

As you whip your manuscript into shape, take a breather and send off a query letter to two or three publishers. Reread Chapter 6, on article writing, to see once again how it is done. But when you write it, make sure it is typed, single-spaced. And don't forget that SASE. You have already learned how important a query letter can be; look through your manuscript, and start your letter with the most intriguing item it contains. Make that editor sit up and pay attention!

In the interim, keep working on your literary endeavor. If you have made too many corrections on a page, redo it. The next time you go shopping, however, find a stationery shop and look for something called "typing correction film." Eberhard and Faber's brand, White Pearl, comes in small boxes of plastic sheets, which are shiny on one side and opaque on the other. Whenever I make a mistake in typing, I slip one of the sheets between the ribbon and page, making sure that the shiny side faces me. I type the wrong letter again, and presto! it disappears and I can type in the correct one. Far too often other kinds of correction sheets leave a residue of white chalk. Whoever invented this kind deserves a medal.

After your manuscript has been typed and you've made your corrections, check it for spelling errors and punctuation. You may have been a whiz at spelling in eighth grade, but this skill has a way of deteriorating as the years gallop along. For example, five of these twenty words are misspelled. Can you find them?

abbreviate	wholely
garantee	marriageable
occurrence	dinosaur
truely	arguement
saccharin	idiosyncrasy
similar	development
harrassment	amateur
feasible	acquire
picnicking	grammar
competent	eccentric

The five misspelled words are: guarantee, truly, harassment, wholly, and argument. If you had trouble finding them, don't be too concerned. You can do what I suggested earlier: pick up a small paperback at the bookstore that contains only spelling words arranged alphabetically.

If you are rather shaky about your grammar, look through your *Elements of Style* by Strunk and White. Don't expect to be a topnotch grammarian overnight. If you are in a dither once in a while over a fine point and can't find an answer anywhere, call your reference librarian or nearby college and see if they know about "Dial-a-Grammarian." Some of the states have this telephone service, and it may now be in your area. But just in case it isn't, you can now dial the Grammar Hotline in California. Dr. Michael Strumpf and his assistants at Moorpark Community College in Ventura County are there to answer all kinds of questions. Call (805)529-2321 9 a.m. to noon, PCT, Monday through Friday, September to June (this is not a free call).

If you are a little uncertain about your punctuation, you can refer to the following pages. I have rounded up the demons that have plagued my students from time to time. First, let's take a look at quotation marks. Here are some basic rules:

1. Use quotations marks to enclose a direct quote.
   Example: Tom said, "The book is better than the movie."
2. Direct quotes, divided into two parts by an interrupting expression (he or she said), require quotation marks around both parts. The second part begins with a small letter if it is part of the same sentence. If it is not, it begins with a capital.

Example: "Why is it," my mother said, "that you always wait until the last minute to do your homework?"
Example: "Be careful going down those stairs," Aunt Emma warned. "They are very rickety."

3. Commas and periods are always placed inside closing quotation marks.

Example: The teacher read aloud "The Raven," a poem by Edgar Allan Poe.

4. Colons and semicolons are always placed outside the closing quotation marks.

Example: The little girl cried, "It's mine"; the little boy ran away.

5. Use single quotation marks to enclose a quotation within a quotation.

Example: "Didn't you hear me ask 'Where is the key?' " she inquired.

If you have forgotten some of the rules of capitalization, here are a few worth knowing:

1. Capitalize the first and important words in a title. It is not necessary to do so with *a, an,* and *the,* or prepositions and conjunctions.

Example: *The Charge of the Light Brigade.* Secretary of the Navy. Colonel James Potter.

2. Capitalize sections of the country; they are not capitalized when they indicate direction.

Example: I will be driving through the Middle West this summer.

Example: Her house is south of town and difficult to find.

3. Do not capitalize the names of seasons unless personified.

Example: I think spring is the best season of all.

Example: Here is Spring in all her glory.

4. Do not capitalize words like theater, hotel, and high school unless they are part of a proper name.

Example: Yorktown High School   a high school student
         Shoreham Hotel   a hotel in Washington

Finally, here are some of the other trouble makers in whipping up a good manuscript:

1. The number of the subject is not changed by a phrase following the subject.

Example: One of the boys is coming to work today.
Example: A knowledge of rules helps the student to use his English correctly.

2. The following pronouns are singular: each, either, neither, one, anyone, everybody, no one, nobody, anyone, someone, and somebody.

Example: Neither girl has the right answer.

3. The following pronouns are plural: few, several, many, both.

Example: Several of these plants are in need of water and special care.

4. The following pronouns may be either singular or plural: all, some, most, any, and none.

Example: Some of the cake was eaten.
          Some of the oranges were eaten.

(Some, most, and all are singular when they refer to a quantity of something and plural when they refer to a number of things thought of individually).

The following sentences contain some demons, too:

1. I can't walk one step *farther*. (Distance)
2. I will not discuss this any *further*. (Distance in abstract ideas)
3. This is strictly between you and *me*. (Between is a preposition and takes a direct object).

Mailing It Out

When you are finally ready to mail out your brainchild, you can fold it into thirds if it's four pages or less, and enclose a long, white SASE. If you have five pages or more, mail them out flat with a thin piece of cardboard enclosed to keep them that way. Buy brown envelopes, which usually come four to a package; the 9x12 size will do nicely. They can be found in a number of stores, including drugstores and supermarkets. Make sure you do not staple your pages; editors pass them around as they read them. Instead, clip them together and make everybody happy.

If you are sending along some illustrations or photographs, make sure that each piece has your name and address lightly penciled in one corner on the back. Mark your envelope DO NOT BEND OR FOLD. Clip your photo or artwork to the cardboard I mentioned before.

When you go to the post office with your precious cargo, you won't know ahead of time how much postage you will need to put on that return envelope, so don't seal your outer one until the clerk has weighed the entire package and you've affixed the necessary postage. You can mail it out FIRST CLASS MAIL or SPECIAL FOURTH CLASS RATE: MANUSCRIPT. First class, of course, costs more, but your manuscript will get better handling and will travel faster. You should be aware that first class mail is forwarded and returned automatically; fourth class is not. To make sure you get your material back if it isn't delivered, print "Return Postage Guaranteed" under your return address.

Should you send a letter along with your submission? The experts advise against it. If, however, there is something you must explain, keep your letter brief and to the point. Don't suffer from the delusion that this bit of correspondence will make your submission look extra special to the editor. Whatever you are sending in will always have to stand on its own merits. If you use fourth class mail, write "First Class Letter Enclosed" on your outside envelope, and pay the extra postage.

When you are mailing out a book manuscript, keep the pages loose, and place them in a flat cardboard box with a cover; a typing paper box is ideal. Reinforce the corners of the box with strapping tape so that it can't fall apart as it goes through the mails. Wrap it in brown mailing paper, and use labels for your addresses; type them neatly so they are readable. It is also wise to print those addresses directly on the package with a black pen in case the labels fall off en route to their destination. It is also a good idea to insure this important package of yours; if it should get lost, you'll have the funds ready for a new typing job. Let me reassure you about manuscripts disappearing: in my twenty years of writing, only one has gone to a distant planet.

Editors have their own pet peeves about manuscripts, and a number of them are in agreement on several that head their list. At the top is neglecting to send a self-addressed stamped envelope; the editor is under no obligation to return material that is not accompanied by that SASE. Another one is sending fiction to a nonfiction publication or the other way around. (You can avoid this by studying the magazine or newspaper you're aiming for, as I have suggested throughout this book.) Another is typing on transparent paper, and using a worn-out ribbon. And one that should be discussed further, sending out multiple submissions.

Multiple Submissions

Now it's one thing to send out a few query letters, but quite another to send out a few copies of an article or short story or book.

It can be embarrassing to get two acceptances at the same time; which one of the editors will you favor? What will you tell the rejected one? If you have never been put in this position before, some friends of mine have. They all admit that it placed them in a quandary. What you can do is read carefully what the editors or publishers will accept. Based on the research I've been doing lately, I can vouch for the fact that a number of book editors are accepting manuscripts that are photocopied, and are going along with the idea of multiple submissions. But I think I can safely say that the majority of editors still expect to receive the original copy of your manuscript, and take it for granted that you have not sent the same version to anyone else. You'll soon see why many writers are becoming impatient with this setup: it's too time-consuming to wait for months before you hear if you have made a sale. But for now it's the right thing to do.

How long should you wait before sending a note to the editor? The consensus seems to be about two months. If you haven't heard by then, type up a short letter in which you ask politely about your article or story or book. Make sure to send a SASE. Just one point: realize that the editor has many other things to do, and also has to make judgments on other submissions.

Copyright

What about copyright? Suppose you have put the finishing touches to a 1,000-word article on a trip to the Bermuda Triangle. You have supplied gems of information that make this article very special. How can you protect it? All you have to do is request the proper form from the Copyright Office. Fill it out, send it along with a $10 registration fee and one copy of your work (two if it's published) to: Register of Copyrights, Library of Congress, Washington, D.C. 20559.

You do not have to register each work individually. A group of articles can be registered at the same time if they meet the following requirements: they must be assembled in orderly fashion by placing them in a notebook binder; they must carry a single title ("Works by Sarah Jones," for example); they must represent the work of one person (or one set of collaborators); and they must be the subject of a single claim of copyright (you cannot claim an individual copyright for each article in the group; for copyright purposes, the group is now a single work). The entire group of articles, by the way, can be registered for $10.

If you want some more information on copyright, write to the same address and ask for their free Copyright Information Kit. This office can answer specific questions, but does not give out any legal advice.

As you go over these tips on how to prepare a manuscript, you are probably impressed with how much is involved. Even if you follow all of them to the letter, there is no guarantee that your work will be bought. But at least you will know that you are putting your best foot forward in the writing world and making a good impression. You're bound to come up a winner sooner or later!

13

You _Can_ Go Home Again

> When I was a boy
> my cousin Marge and I
> became somewhat disturbed
> when Sister Mary Martin told us
> that God watched us constantly,
> day and night, rain or shine.
> I enjoyed company
> but this seemed ridiculous.
> I told my mother the problem
> and she said we might tell a union
> about God's non-union hours.
> Dad said we might tell a priest
> about committing blasphemy.
> Mother said she couldn't spell
> blasphemy,
> much less commit it.
> Then, getting serious, Mother told me
> it was strange that the young
> wished God would look away
> while the old considered it fearful
> that He might look away.
> I thought that was easy for Mother
> and Sister Mary Martin to say
> as both were old—maybe thirty—
> and probably finished sinning.
>
> —Jim Hausman, 1976

If you found yourself chuckling over this bit of material, you can readily see why Jim Hausman's mini-vignettes on nostalgia became syndicated to over sixty newspapers. He kept a journal about his boyhood experiences for many years, and when he retired from the U.S. Air Force in 1963, he returned to his hometown of Cincinnati and began to put his notes together. But it wasn't until 1973 that he finally gathered up his notebooks and marched in—without an appointment—to see the editor of the _Cincinnati Enquirer_.

Brady Black, the man in charge, liked what he read and agreed to use the vignettes as columns twice a week. But it proved to be so popular that he decided to run five a week for his enthusiastic readership. Later on, Jim Hausman's "When I Was a Boy" was syndicated in sixty-three newspapers, and he eventually had a book published based on his columns.

If you have kept a journal or diary for a long time, read it over and see if it could lend itself to a column on nostalgia. But if you've never kept a record of any kind before, start now. It will provide you with a storehouse of information in your years ahead as a writer. It doesn't matter what age you are; the important thing is to get into the habit of putting down on paper your thoughts and observations from day to day.

What exactly is nostalgia? According to the dictionary, it's "a desire to return in thought or in fact to a former time in one's life, to one's home, or to one's family and friends." It must, of course, be associated with emotion and bring back fond memories of long ago. Here are some questions which will take you back in time and make you grab a pencil:

- What games did you play when you were a child? Can you remember Statues or Kick the Can or Run, Sheep, Run, or Cat's Cradle? Can you describe them?

- Who was your favorite teacher? Why? Can you remember the one you didn't like, and the tricks the whole class played on him or her? What was your favorite subject? Who was the worst-behaved boy (or girl) in the class? How was the culprit punished?

- How did you amuse yourself on a rainy day? I can remember curling up with a book and a bag of apples or writing a story or play for the class; I can also remember that what I wrote was more to be pitied than censured.

- Did you grow up in the Beatlemania era? What can you tell us about the trends and customs of that

time? Which songs were your favorites? In this turbu-
lent time frame, what can you remember that can still
be classified as "fond memories"?

- Are you a product of the Roaring Twenties? Can
you remember saying, "Oh, you kid!" or dancing the
Charleston or singing "Bye Bye Blackbird" and "When
Day is Done"? Those were the days, my friend, when
any female in the family was practically condemned
to death if she bobbed her hair. I can remember my
mother telling me she did just that, and that her whole
family looked at her in horror as she walked in the
door. To help you recall such a moment in your life,
read "Bernice Bobs Her Hair" by F. Scott Fitzgerald,
an authority on the twenties.

- Can you take us back to the 1940s and tell us
about the friendships you formed during World War
II? Can you remember some unusual things that happened? Cowan McFarland, a retired colonel who lives
in my area has contacted the medics in his unit during
the war and has recently published a follow-up on the
men in his company. The book contains a kind of nostalgia that will have a great deal of meaning to the soldiers who were in combat together many years ago.

Holiday Memories

Probably one of the easiest ways to reminisce is to think about
Christmases past. Walter Olesky, who writes for *Modern Maturity*
magazine, interviewed a number of celebrities in 1979, and asked
them to think about a Christmas they would never forget. They
responded with a variety of answers, and here are some excerpts:

> *Lillian Gish:* When I was five years old and touring on the
> road with a melodrama, Christmas found our company in
> Detroit. . . . One of the cast members asked me what I wanted
> Santa to bring me, and I replied, "A comb, a mirror, and
> a muff."

Christmas fell on a Saturday, and between matinee and evening performances, some men came backstage and asked to take me across the alley to an automobile agency. In the center of their showroom was an enormous Christmas tree, and under it, three brightly wrapped packages.

When I opened them, I found a comb, a mirror, and a muff. . . .

James Roosevelt: My favorite Christmas was the first time I was allowed to join the family and hear my father read "A Christmas Carol." He not only read it to his children . . . but later to his grandchildren.

Lawrence Welk: All my Christmases were memorable! I can still remember vividly how my seven brothers and sisters and I would wait with anguished anticipation for the arrival of St. Nicholas on the night before Christmas. All eight of us would perch rigidly on the edge of our chairs in the kitchen, waiting anxiously for the sound of sleigh bells outside.

The moment we heard the sleigh bells, Father would fling open the door—and there he'd be, St. Nicholas himself, all rosy and red, garbed in a scarlet suit with white whiskers flowing down over his ample chest, a big smile on his face, a twinkle in his eye—and a dreaded question on his lips:

"Have you boys and girls been good little boys and girls this year?" . . .

George Burns: Doesn't it seem strange to be asking Jewish people about the Christmas they'll never forget? I came from a very poor and very large family. My family was raised as Orthodox, so Christmas was not our holiday, but Hanukkah was almost the equivalent. The Hanukkah I'll never forget is the one when for a present I got one roller skate. That's right, just one skate. I think it fit either foot, and where it came from, I don't know. Come to think of it, I never did get the other one.

(*Modern Maturity,* 1979-1980)

Is there a Christmas that stands out in your mind? Or a special Thanksgiving? Accounts of these two holidays must be different and outstanding to impress the editor of a newspaper or magazine. You may have more luck in getting an acceptance to try remembering a Fourth of July or a terrifying Halloween from the past. But I did come across a Christmas story recently that had a touch of whimsy about it which made it delightful to read. A freelancer by the name of Floyce Larson told about the Christmas when her Norwegian grandmother visited her Wisconsin farm and related the old legend about the animals speaking on Christmas morning. As the two of them baked some bread for the animals on the farm, Floyce was tempted to mention the fact that she had tried on her mother's gold ring and that it had somehow come off her finger. She searched all over and couldn't find it anywhere. We pick up her story on Christmas Eve:

> After church, we all stayed up later than usual. We sat around the kitchen table drinking hot chocolate and eating popcorn while sister made fudge on the old wood cooking stove.
>
> It was almost midnight when I finally lit the kerosene lantern and headed for the barn with my basket. I had loaves of rye, pumpernickel, whole wheat, corn muffins and even some raised potato donuts.
>
> The sleeping animals came alive when they heard me. I tore off chunks of dark rye for the cows and gave portions to pigs who grunted their approval. Lambs nuzzled my basket and each received a corn muffin . . .
>
> For Prince, the horse, I saved a special loaf of whole wheat . . . Something about him caught my attention. Staring at me in a strange manner, he opened his mouth. I would have sworn on my Confirmation Bible that I heard him say:
>
> "Seek again."
>
> Something compelled me to hang the lantern on a hook as I looked at the pile of hay. There, glinting like a star was the precious gold ring . . . So far as I know, Prince never spoke again.
>
> I left home a few years after that special, magical night. But whenever I returned while Prince was still alive, I went out to the barn to pay him a visit. As I patted him on the nose

and offered him a little treat, it seemed he gave me a knowing nod. And always, some mystical feeling passed between us.

(*Washington Post*, December 24, 1980)

The Historical Angle

If you are a history buff, your nostalgia articles or fillers can take a different turn and give the reader a fascinating account of what it was like to live many years ago. For example, one of my students wrote up a kind of "You Are There" article on fourth graders visiting the home of Robert E. Lee in Arlington. She was especially interested in the project because her daughter was one of the students. Shelby Lawrence described what it was like to live in a white-pillared mansion in Virginia more than 150 years ago. She then told about the children being received on the mansion's commanding portico by a gracious hoop-skirted lady and going on a tour of the house. After learning some facts about the Lee family, the students were divided into four groups. A short time later . . .

A heavenly smell soon drifts from the kitchen where the young cooks are baking battercakes which they will devour with honey. In the greenhouse, hands start cuttings and bulbs on a new life. At the same time, a kindly gentleman in woolen workclothes prowls the grounds, the cellar, and the attic with his group, noting how native materials were transformed into the handsome neo-Grecian dwelling. In the attic, the fourth group of students digs into trunks filled with waves of taffeta and crinoline. Before long, several 20th-century girls are transformed into giggling Southern belles. There on a table, crocks hold herbs and spices to be ground for sachets.

(*Arlington News*, June 14, 1972)

Shelby ended her short feature by saying that when this trip into the past was finished, each student was reluctant to board the bus and return to the present. The members of my writing class enjoyed her story, and she had it published in a local paper.

Repasts of the Past

The kitchen of long ago seems to be a focal point for many nostalgia pieces these days, and one that I found appealing was written by Goody Solomon, a columnist for the *Fairfax Journal*. She described her mother's 1930s kitchen in New York City where she grew up and told about coming home from school and finding her mother chopping chicken livers, koshering meats, or scrubbing and polishing. She also recalled how important it was to have fresh vegetables every day in her household and to have balanced and nutritious meals. She emphasized that her mother didn't even own a cookbook, but managed to turn out appetizing food. The lengthy column also revealed that prepackaged items were frowned upon and good meant fresh foods, carefully chosen and prepared. Goody's mother believed in steaming string beans, baking or boiling potatoes, and broiling meats and fish. Goody's own interest in food and nutrition probably stems from those early days.

Did you ever go to a general store when you were growing up? How about taking us there and sharing with us some of the atmosphere and the goodies you found there? If your memory needs a bit of jogging, here are some things which will help you go back in time: wooden counters and cases; a vintage cash register; a potbellied stove; a working post office that hand-cancels mail with its own stamp; shelves crowded with baskets; craft books; brooms; stuffed calico cats; posters; dolls. And don't forget those glass jugs chock-full of penny candy: jawbreakers, fruit slices, and licorice twists. Add your own little remembrances and write up an article that will make us wistful for that special store.

Did you have a grandmother who was known for her home remedies? A writer by the name of Mai Thomas did, and in 1975 she had a book published that contained a number of her granny's health hints. Here are some from the turn of the century (Granny warned not to try any of them without consulting a doctor):

ARTHRITIS: Take one tablespoon of liquid Certo in a glass of cranberry juice every morning.

DIURETIC: Boil about a cup of watermelon or sunflower seeds in a quart of water. Strain to make hot tea.

WARTS: Cut white potato in half. Rub with juice of potato.

COUGH: Lemon juice, honey, and whiskey.

FACING SURGERY: Week or two before, start having some jello every day.

(Granny's Remedies, Gramercy Publishing)

Food also plays an important role in thinking about the past. Mimi Sheraton wrote an article on memories of hot cereal mornings that without a doubt made many readers recall winter mornings when they were children, and fervently wished they could stay under the covers instead of getting up for school. What really helped in facing the morning was the thought of a bowl of steaming hot cereal and cream. The author whets our appetite with:

> If the rest of the world presented a foreboding frost-white picture, the kitchen at least was a fragrant, steaming center of warmth and well-being.
>
> Coffee was perking for grown-ups, perhaps cocoa was simmering for children, cinnamon toast might be gilding under the broiler, and the sharp, tropical scent of freshly sliced oranges added a reminder of summer. A peek into the burbling pot told us which cereal was on the daily menu and, if memory serves correctly, my mother kept a regular store of a dozen or so varieties.
>
> . . . As much as I loved the creamy cereals the day they were cooked, I adored them even more the second day, when leftover "mush" was cut into squares and slowly fried in butter until both sides were golden brown.
>
> *(New York Times* Company, 1978)

This article ran about 1,000 words and followed all the rules of good writing. Sheraton used specifics whenever possible so that we could smell and see and taste those breakfasts. And whenever she did use an adjective, she made it count. Some of her verbs also added special effects: perking. . . simmering. . . gilding.

Other Sources of Inspiration

Muriel Dryden, a friend of mine and a student in one of my classes, did a nostalgia filler a few months ago that should motivate some of you to write about the same subject. She comes from Iowa, and for a long time she has wanted to write about a shivaree. Here is her description:

> The shivaree custom was observed in midwestern states from early in the twentieth century through the depression

years. When a wedding date was announced, word traveled quickly among the young people of the community. On the evening of the wedding day, we gathered near the bride's family home where the newlyweds were expected to spend their nuptial night. Cars weren't plentiful then and wages were so low that almost no one ever left for a honeymoon. As darkness fell, we would sneak quietly down the street to secure the surprise element in the shivaree ritual, althought I'm sure every couple expected us.

When everyone had gathered around the house, the shivaree began. All took part in banging kettles or pans brought from home, playing combs, drawing sticks along the fence or whistling. The noise might be likened to that made by musicians tuning their instruments. This went on for about ten minutes until someone led a chant: "Come out, come out, before we drag you out!" Finally, the shy, giggling bride and groom appeared on the porch, whereupon they were bombarded with cheers and rice.

(_Senior Scribes,_ October 1980)

Have you ever fallen in love with a city? A freelance writer by the name of Laura Holz did that very thing and wrote a letter to Washington, D.C., expressing her thought. I'm constantly amazed at the creativity of some people, and must admit that I would never have come up with this unique idea for a nostalgia piece:

Dear Washington:

This is a love letter to you, as I knew you almost 60 years ago, when I was young, and you were a small southern city on the Potomac.

I remember band concerts at Dupont Circle. We would sit on the wooden park benches or walk the circular paths, listening to the music while a golden summer moon made patterns on the grass.

Afterwards, we would stroll down Connecticut Avenue looking in windows at treasures beyond our pocketbooks. That avenue was a quiet street then, where nursemaids in uniform pushed English prams and old ladies in electric automobiles went shopping in the afternoon.

On a spring morning at Connecticut Avenue and S Street you could hear the organ grinder's music: "My little girl, you know I love you, and I long for you each day," or "Goodbye, My Lady Love."

I remember the old Ebbit House, on the corner of 14th and F Streets, with a small, shaded lamp on each little table. For a quarter you could sit and drink heavenly coffee, served with little sweet cakes, while a small string orchestra played chamber music.

Can anyone who knew the Washington of those days ever forget "Herbert's" on 19th Street near the Avenue? For 35 cents you were served the most delectable, tender veal cutlet with tomato sauce, mashed potatoes, hot biscuits, and coffee.

For dessert, there was always the agonizing dilemma of devil's food cake, two luscious chocolate layers, piled high with thick marshmallow filling, or your choice of apple or blueberry pie, with a flaky crust.

On Saturday night we would ride the trolley out to Chevy Chase Lake or Glen Echo and dance until they dimmed the lights, and the musicians packed away their instruments. We would rush for the last street car, always an open one in the summertime.

We would sit on the rear seats singing the old songs: "My Old Kentucky Home" and "Moonlight Bay."

If we had money to spare, we went to the movies and thrilled over Theda Bara or William S. Hart, our western hero. . . .

During the day we worked hard. We all had what we considered good jobs. Most of us were comfortably housed and fed. True, a lot of us lived in furnished rooms, but our salaries seemed adequate if we were careful.

At night the city was our playground. It was a gentle city, and no matter where we lived, there was no thought of danger.

This, then, was you, Washington, long ago when I was young, as I knew you and loved you and will always remember you.

(*Washington Star*, September 1974)

Do you have a flair for writing doggerel verse? I found the

following poem at Culpepper Garden. No one claimed to be its author and it needs a better ending, but someone had fun doing these lines:

Remember when Hippie applied to your hips,
And a Trip involved travel in cars, planes, and ships,
When Neat meant well-organized, tidy, and clean,
And Grass was ground cover that grew tall and green,
When Fuzz was a substance as fluffy as lint,
And Bread came from bakeries, not from the mint,
When Roll meant a bun, and Rock was a stone,
And Hang-Up was something you did to a phone,
When Swinger was someone who swings on a swing,
And Pad was a soft sort of cushiony thing,
When Dig meant to shovel and spade in the dirt,
And Put-On was what you did to a shirt.

As I mentioned in an earlier chapter, nostalgia is "in," and if you can choose some phase of it, you will probably find a market for your material. Some of the big-name writers are doing some reminiscing of their own; I especially enjoyed an article done by Pete Hamill, a New York-based writer, at the beginning of 1981. He would like to bring back the past and return to the summer of 1957 when the Dodgers were in Brooklyn and the Giants in the Polo Grounds; he wants all menus written in English, not French; he longs for the return of double features along with cartoons and coming attractions; he wants doctors to make house calls again; he'd like to hear Latin again in the Roman Catholic mass; and he'd like the return of men who know how to fix things.

When you have chosen your topic for your nostalgia filler or article or poem, you can round it out by spending some time at the library. Look for a book called *The American Encyclopedia of Dates and Facts*; it will supply you with background material for the time frame you have chosen. It will even give you the names of songs that were popular then. *The People's Almanac* will also give you the same kind of information. You may be interested in looking up old newspapers on microfilm; check with the reference librarian. You may also want to ask her about the nostalgia kits now appearing in libraries across the country. There are four available in my town: "Remembering the Depression," "Remembering School Days," "Remembering 1924," and "Remembering Train Rides." In these kits are cassette tapes, slides in carousels, and skits with appropriate props.

Enjoy your trip down Memory Lane!

14

Of Cabbages and Kings

"The time has come," the Walrus said,
    "To talk of many things:
Of shoes—and ships—and sealing wax—
    Of cabbages—and kings—
And why the sea is boiling hot—
    And whether pigs have wings."

—Lewis Carroll

This chapter will cover all kind of writings that won't make an appearance on the commercial market. I'm sure there are some of you who would like to do an autobiography for your children and grandchildren that is more than a family tree. I believe there are a number of you who'd like some ideas on putting material together for your own edification or satisfaction. And there must be a few of you who wonder if letter writing is really a lost art. The ideas presented in this last segment of the book have been gleaned from many of my friends who are also looking for ways to leave a special legacy, or want to write just for the sake of writing.

Quotation Collections

If you have been collecting bits of poetry, jokes, quips, famous sayings, some lines from a book, or thoughts on life itself, how about buying something like *The Nothing Book*? There is such a thing, believe it or not, published by Harmony Books in New York, and it contains blank pages. Its blurb reads:

> When asked what five books he would take with him to a desert island, George Bernard Shaw replied that he would take five blank books . . . We have bound together 192 sheets of fine paper. The possibilities are endless. Write your own novel, compile a personal cookbook, draw pictures, make lists, keep records, collect autographs, write poetry, plan vacations, start a diary or scrapbook, design clothes, invent needlework or knitting patterns, doodle, compose songs, jot down impor-

> tant dates, keep a guest book, press flowers, gather favorite
> quotes, accumulate (or invent) funny stories, use your imagi-
> nation and do your own thing.

If you check department stores or bookshops, you should be able to find a reasonable facsimile.

I found out about this publication when I attended a writers' meeting several weeks ago. As I looked around the table, there sat Frances reading something that had a white cover with the word "Nothing" on it in big letters. Of course I had to ask her a few questions, and she told me that she had owned it for several years, and that it was filled with her favorite items. She elaborated a bit more, and gave me the following:

- A quote from H. L. Mencken: "The Puritan is one who is afraid that somewhere, somehow, someone is having a good time."
- A poem by Muhammad Ali during a speech at the New School for Social Research in New York City:
  Stay in college
  Get the knowledge
  Stay there till you're through.
  If they can make
  Penicillin out of moldy bread—
  They can sure make something out of you.
- A quote from her friend Hazel: "When someone says 'Don't go to Paris, Hazel, you'll get pinched,' I always tell them I'll just turn the other cheek."

Frances also told me about gathering quotes from Ruth Gordon, Woody Allen, Thornton Wilder, Ingrid Bergman, and Ogden Nash, and including some of her own poetry. She is constantly on the lookout for a variety of material for her book, and enjoys this kind of writing and collecting. Eventually, it will wend its way to her son and her grandchildren.

What five books would you take with you if you went to a desert island? When George Bernard Shaw was asked this question many years ago, he said that he would take five blank books. Maybe your answer wouldn't be quite the same, but he wanted to emphasize that a writer can create his own diversions by jotting down his thoughts or making up certain storylines. But your blank book could be filled with those quotes you are always collecting whether you are reading fiction or nonfiction; those sketches you do whenever you sit out under that old oak in the backyard; those anecdotes you tell at parties; the talks that you give at the club meetings; the things that your children do and say; those secret family recipes you've been gathering for years, etc. You already have a head start on keeping a blank book of your own. All you have to do is take all those notes you've scribbled on the backs of envelopes or grocery lists and put them in a much better place.

I've already started to gather snippets of this and snippets of that for the blank book I'll buy very soon. Lesley Conger, a columnist for *The Writer*, enjoys scribbling in her book, and likes the change of pace from clacking away at her typewriter most of the time. She calls it her "commonplace" book, and at first I thought she made up the word. But there is such a word in the dictionary; it's defined as "a book in which noteworthy quotations, poems, comments, etc., are written."

I've singled out a few items I've been saving for a long time, and when you read them, I think you'll be able to see why they are special to me. The first one is a poem written by John Magee, Jr., who was born in Shanghai of missionary parents and enlisted in the Royal Canadian Air Force at the outbreak of World War II. He was shot down shortly after he wrote this; I find it especially poignant because he was only nineteen when he was killed in action. Here are his lines:

High Flight

Oh, I have slipped the surly bonds of earth,
And danced the skies on laughter-silvered wings;
Sunward I've climbed and joined the tumbling mirth
Of sun-split clouds—and done a hundred things
You have not dreamed of—wheeled and soared and swung
High in the sunlit silence. Hov'ring there,
I've chased the shouting wind along and flung
My eager craft through footless halls of air.
Up, up the long delirious, burning blue
I've topped the wind-swept heights with easy grace,

Where never lark, or even eagle, flew;
And, while with silent, lifting mind I've trod
The high untrespassed sanctity of space,
Put out my hand, and touched the face of God.
     (Reprinted by permission of the Canadian Air Force)

There are two quotes I cherish and they are:

A friend is someone who knows all about you and loves
you just the same.

—Elbert Hubbard

My Heart is warm with
the friends I make.

—Edna St. Vincent Millay

There is an Irish saying that will also find its way into my
commonplace book:

May ye enter the gates of heaven a half hour before the
Devil knows you're dead.

I've collected a number of Irish poems that I'll include in my
commonplace book, but the one I especially like is a kind of toast
or blessing, and one that you might recognize. The lines are:

May the road rise to meet you,
May the wind be always at your back,
May the sun shine warm upon your face,
And until we meet again—
May God hold you in the hollow of His hand.

This material that I've described on the last few pages tells you
only one way to do a commonplace book. But there isn't any reason
why you can't include some sayings of your children or grandchildren along with your literary observations. I may decide to
write down the time when one of my sons asked, "Do pickles come
from alligators?" or include a poem or drawing of two of my granddaughters' that were published a few years ago. But once again,
there isn't any reason why you can't keep several books, and keep
them separate from each other.

The Scrapbook

Do you have a number of clippings on hand that you have saved through the years? You may want to do a kind of scrapbook. Inez Whitney, a retired schoolteacher from Oklahoma, has a memento from her mother that will give you some ideas along this line. It's called "Mama's Scrapbook," and dates back to 1898. (What surprised me about it is the fact that even then she wrote her favorite things in the blank pages of an 8x10 hardcover book like the one I have just described.) What's in it? It's a potpourri of information, but most of it deals with items that involve Inez's family. There are clippings from the *Custer Courier* that mention the return of Inez's uncle from the Civil War; a letter written by Inez to Santa Claus when she was seven or eight; obituaries of her family and friends; and write-ups on some of the prizes and accolades bestowed on Inez in her school days. But Mama had ideas of her own, and included a family register of dates and births; colorful picture postcards; the names of her grandfathers and her great-grandfathers; magazine pictures of cute children; and religious poems.

One of the items in it was a ballad that is fun to read, a bit of nostalgia that sets the scene for life in America seventy or eighty years ago. The ballad reads:

> A gay and handsome traveling man lay on a bed of pain,
> All hope had passed, his life went fast, he'd never rise again;
> "Hast thou no sweetheart, fair and true?" they whispered o'er
> his bed,
> "Whom thou wouldst tell a last farewell?" The young man
> softly said:
> "There's Daisy back in Lexington, and Nellie at Cordell;
> There's Millie down in Normantown, and Mary in Purcel.
> And at Shawnee there's Esther, dear, whom I must surely see.
> And Anna, too, at Mountain View, please bring them all to
> me."
> The watchers started with mild surprise, and then they said
> once more,
> "Come tell us pray, without delay, the girl whom you adore;
> The girl whom you have sworn to love and bring both wealth
> and fame;

> Your promised wife, your hope and life, quick, let us hear her
>   name."
> "There's Maggie out at Sayre," he said, "and Pearl at El Reno,
> There's Violet at Calumet, and Maude at old Hydro;
> And Genevieve at Hennessey, and Mable at Mulhall."
> The young man sighed, "It's time I died, I swore to wed them
>   all!"

Genealogical Writing

Is this the year you are determined to shake your family tree and trace your roots? Alex Haley, of course, started this trend several years ago, and if you have never done anything like this before, you'll find it very rewarding. Listen to this short account written by a student in one of my classes who has worked in this field:

Have You Tried Genealogy?

by

Florence Campbell

Did you know that ten generations back in your ancestry there are 1,024 great-great-great-great-great-great-great-grandparents? But more recently, do you know the maiden names of your four great-grandmothers?

Give genealogy a try. Check your public library for "how-to" books; try the daytime or evening courses in genealogy conducted free of charge or for a small fee.

At the National Archives in Washington, I found the pension file of a great-grandfather who fought in the War of 1812, and who for this military service was granted 160 acres of land in the wilds of Minnesota in 1857. He was by that time 64 years of age and living in Canada, and in no way could homestead there, so he sold the land to a "squatter" for about $200. I also learned he was tall, blond, and blue-eyed, as great-grandmother described. I recently found that a great-grandmother's five brothers and sisters migrated from Calais, Maine, to northern California in the 1860's, and are recorded as among the earliest pioneers in the redwood country. To get there, some journeyed by sailing ship around Cape Horn to

Humboldt Bay in California. Others sailed to the Isthmus of Panama, crossed by mule team to the Pacific, and continued via ship to California. Four-masted schooners, the Isthmus of Panama, lumbering in redwood country, and New England farmers who became California ranchers—history, geography, genealogy!

My research led me to membership in the DAR three years ago, and this introduced me to many fascinating bits of history. Did you know there are two DAR chapters in France? The Regent of one chapter is a countess! The members are descendants of men who came to the colonies to fight with General Lafayette, and these chapters open each meeting with a champagne toast.

Visit the National Archives, and look at the 1900 census records. You may find your great-grandfather's Civil War pension file, or the lists of ships' passengers arriving at United States ports. You will be amazed at the information you'll uncover here.

Try genealogy. Become a detective, a history buff, a biographer, or just a plain old snoop!

Now that you have read this teaser on genealogy, you may find yourself motivated to do some research on your own family. I felt the same way after I read Florence's write-up in the *Senior Scribes* newsletter, but didn't quite know where to begin. My research on the subject provided a wealth of information, but I finally sifted through the details and came up with these guidelines:

1. The first thing to do is to choose only one line of your family; your surname will fit the bill.
2. Then search in your home and relatives' homes for the names, dates, and places of birth of your grandfather and great-grandfather, going back as far as you can. Look in the family Bible, journals, diaries, etc., for all of this information.
3. Next on the agenda should be a visit to your oldest living relatives. Ask them from which country your ancestors came, and the dates of their births, marriages, and deaths.

4. The next step is to check the public records. If you know that your grandfather came from Fairfax County, Virginia, you would obtain copies of his birth certificate and marriage license from the courthouse there. In order to do so, you would need his name and the approximate year of the event. You can get booklets from the U.S. Government Printing Office, Superintendent of Documents, Washington, D.C. 20402, that will help you in locating their certificates. Ask for "Where to Write for Birth and Death Certificates" or "Where to Write for Marriage Records." Each one costs 35¢ at the present time.

5. County courthouses have records that contain wills, marriage licenses, death certificates, and land records.

6. Local undertakers have records that also have helpful information: the date your relative died, names of his nearest relatives, and place of burial. If you go to the cemetery, you could find the graves of his parents and the dates of their births and deaths.

7. Get in contact with the National Archives in Washington, D.C., which can provide you with a storehouse of facts about your ancestors. Their records of the national census taken every ten years since 1790 provide such valuable data as the names of everyone in the household, the year they immigrated to America, and their origins. You can also obtain information on military and pension records by sending for their pamphlet on this subject (include SASE). Their address is: The National Archives and Records Service, General Services Administration, Washington, D.C. 20408.

If you are interested in seeing the passenger list of certain ships, ask for their Form GSA-7111. This list will tell you when your immigrant relative arrived in America, and the country he came from.

If you decide to trace your ancestors in the country from which they came, contact the library of the Church of Jesus Christ of Latter-Day Saints, Salt Lake City, Utah 84150. It holds information on people of every race, creed, and nationality from more than forty countries.

And you probably already know that the Library of Congress and the Daughters of the American Revolution have much to offer if you come to Washington some day. In the meantime, check into these books at your library for more details:

A Guide to Genealogical Research by Esther Williams
Searching for Your Ancestors by Gilbert H. Doane
The Researcher's Guide to American Genealogy by V. Greenwood

There are a number of paperbacks about genealogy on the market now, and you may wish to buy one or two as you become a sleuth. If you can't find the following titles at your bookstore or at the library, I've included the publisher's address:

Tracing, Charting, and Writing Your Family History ($2.50) by Lois Skalka. Pilot Books, 347 Fifth Ave., New York, NY 10006.

Who Do You Think You Are? ($1.75) by Suzanne Hilton. Signet Books (The New American Library), 1301 Avenue of the Americas, New York, NY 10019.

As you begin to shake your family tree, don't be shook up by what will come down. So what if a pirate suddenly comes to life or a jilted bride pops up? One of Florence Campbell's neighbors found an ancestor who had written a gothic novel in 1876 called Elmwood, or The Withered Arm, and it still can create a mood of impending doom. An excerpt reads:

> . . . A wild, unearthly yell broke with fearful distinction on the midnight silence. Trembling in every joint, my hair standing on my head, my blood suddenly frozen in my veins, I sprang wildly to my feet, listening for a repetition of that horrible cry. But it came not. Suddenly, a thought flashed through my bewildered mind. I flew to the great gloomy bedstead, which, with its antique canopy and heavy drapery more than once reminded me of a hearse. It was empty! She was gone! . . .

This book was written by someone who called herself Katie L., and was published by a company in Baltimore. You must admit that her descendants today feel that they know her a little bit better because of her story. When you do your research on who begat whom, try to add some extra touches or family folklore that will make your ancestors sound more real. Your library will have some books on this subject; ask the reference librarian. You can also obtain a booklet called "Family Folklore" (#047-000-00352-1) for $1 from the U.S. Government Printing Office, Superintendent of Documents, 732 N. Capitol St. N.W., Washington, D.C. 20402.

Right now I'm doing some research of my own and will note that my mother's father sang and played the guitar, and had the lightheartedness of a gypsy. I never knew him, so I will have to take my mother's word for it. I've also learned that my father's mother came from a long line of McCarthys, and they may have been related to the McCarthys who built and lived in Blarney Castle in County Cork. Maybe. And I also plan to record that my Bavarian grandmother's sweet and sour red cabbage has been a tradition in my family for eighty years—and will go on and on and on. My grandchildren will never let it disappear from their holiday dinners.

Letters

If you have written all kinds of letters through the years, you may want to collect them from your friends and relatives and place them in a scrapbook. I know a husband and wife who are trying to do that very thing, and another couple who are currently going over thirty years of letters they have sent at Christmas time. While there may be gaps in the sequence, letters are in a way a kind of autobiography and depict a person's character, his hopes and his disappointments. They also tell something about life in America, and how changes come about from decade to decade.

When E. B. White was contacted by one of his editors in 1972 who asked if she could collect his letters written over a long period of time, he told her he didn't consider himself a letter writer. But he thought about it, and discovered that his wife had saved many of his letters dating back to the twenties and thirties. His editor combined her collection with Mrs. White's, and a book was born. When you have a spare moment, read *The Letters of E. B. White;* you'll feel as though you are listening to a friend.

Have you ever received letters from camp? See if you can find them. If you dig up only a handful, how about putting them together with other letters written by your children? You may want to do a sketch or two; take a look at Bill Adler's book called *Letters from Camp*. A scrapbook of this kind will help you recall some of the happiest moments of your life. It will also be a most unusual gift to your son or daughter later on.

Muriel Dryden, a friend of mine, felt a need to keep in touch with the younger generation of her family, and initiated a letter exchange. At the outset, their mothers assisted with replies. Through the years, she kept a box for each writer's letters which enabled her to watch them grow up even though they were in Iowa and she was in New York and Washington, D.C. At the end of twenty years, she put each set into a binder along with some snapshots and added a preface in which she shared her thoughts, and the pleasures received from the correspondence. At a memorable family Christmas gathering, the collections were handed over to her nephews and nieces, who were thrilled to see the letters they had written over the years.

Representative William Natcher of Kentucky has written a letter every week to his six grandsons and one granddaughter for the past fourteen years. In each envelope he includes their weekly allowance, ranging from $2 to $10, according to their various ages. In every letter, he tries to tell something interesting about the nation's capital so they can learn some history in a palatable way. He recently said that one letter his grandchildren enjoyed reading centered around John Quincy Adams's diary that told about skinny-dipping in the Potomac River.

As I mentioned before, letters have a way of telling us things about a person that we would never have known from his other writings or interviews. If you've become known for your sparkling communications with your family and friends keep up the good work. Letter writing is an art form that mustn't be lost.

Writing Your Autobiography

Would you like to write your autobiography? If you have kept a diary or a journal, your task won't be too formidable. If you haven't, start now to outline the events of your life. You can get some help by digging out old family albums and studying the pictures. Use your tape recorder to collect stories from family and friends. Take a look at old newspapers to see what was happening on the day you were born, graduated from high school or college, or were married. And don't forget to use *The Encyclopedia of American Facts and Dates* to help you recall the popular songs during those years.

There is a book called *How to Write the Story of Your Life* written by Frank P. Thomas that can provide you with all of the details on how to put an autobiography together. You should be able to find it at your library. If not, write to Writer's Digest Books, 9933 Alliance Rd., Cincinnati, OH 45242.

I would suggest that before you do any serious writing, you read some of the following autobiographies:

>   *Changing* by Liv Ullman
>   *Dear Me* by Peter Ustinov
>   *Waiting for the Morning Train* by Bruce Catton
>   *On Reflection* by Helen Hayes
>   *The Moon's a Balloon* by David Niven
>   *At Ease* by Dwight D. Eisenhower
>   *All Creatures Great and Small* by James Herriot
>   *All the Strange Hours* by Loren Eisely
>   *Living It Up* by George Burns
>   *Roses in December* by Frances Parkinson Keyes
>   *Haywire* by Brooke Hayward
>   *History of My Life* by Casanova
>   *Don't Fall Off the Mountain* by Shirley MacLaine
>   *Lauren Bacall By Myself* by Lauren Bacall

Some of these books were done by professional writers, but several were done by people not in the writing field. Keep in mind that you are writing the story of your life for your satisfaction and as a legacy for your family; you are not looking for a publisher. But if you want your material to have a polished look, thumb through the books I've listed to see what approach each of them used.

The day may come when you may decide to have a book printed at your own expense. A guest speaker at one of my classes, Edward Beitzell, wrote *Life on the Potomac* after doing research on the area in which he lived. It all started when he became interested in genealogy; his search led him to so much information that he simply had to write it all down. Since that time, he has written several more history books, which seem to sell on a steady basis.

Those of you who have served in the military will be interested in a project undertaken by Cowan McFarland, a retired colonel. He has been gathering material for a book that will be of sentimental value to the men who were in his company years ago. Here is part of his preface:

> This is a story about field medical soldiers. It is a collection of their words—words about their experiences, their adventures, their gripes, and their hopes. It is also a collection of historical and personal narrative, of soldier poetry and humor.
>
> It is presented here essentially as we wrote it in 1945, deep in eastern Germany at the end of a military adventure that began in the pine woods at Camp Shelby, Mississippi, and ended in the war-devastated region at Leipzig, Germany.
>
> It is also a story of one infantry divisional medical collecting company: Company A, 369th Medical Battalion, 69th Infantry Division—its birth, its growth, its combat experiences and attainments, and its deactivation. In essence, it is a record of the men, their company, and their experiences.
>
> Because many of our buddies have answered the call of taps, I am sorry that I did not complete this project many years ago. It would have been rewarding for them to have shared these pages with their loved ones. I regret so much the delay; however, I must act from where I am, and I hope that perhaps this effort will atone for the long gap between writing and printing, and that these pages will bring joy, reminiscence, and a sense of comradeship to those of us who "continue the march!"
>
> As our approach toward making a lasting contribution with this story of our wartime experiences, copies of *Shelby to the Elbe* have been added to the libraries of the United States Army Center of Military History, Washington, D.C., and the United States Army Military History Institute, Carlisle Barracks, Pa., thus being melded with volumes of other soldiers' stories.

The material gathered by Colonel McFarland is now at the printer's, and before long, bound books will be sent to about forty men from Company A. (Please note that they are not being done by a publisher; this is strictly a noncommercial enterprise.) You can see that a book of this kind will provide a unique legacy, and one that other family members will cherish.

I think I would be remiss if I didn't discuss your doing a diary or journal. If you desire to do a "Dear Diary" kind of recording, do it. Make it personal; make that book your confidant, and tell how you feel after a walk in the woods; an argument with your spouse; seeing a sunset; the condition of the country; your new love; your daughter's marriage; your first grandchild; your trip to Hawaii; the death of your cat; a special poem; a gripping novel; a storm brewing.

But if you want a kind of book in which you can write down your thoughts and observations pertaining to writing, you can check into the *Writer's Digest Diary*, which is fairly new on the scene. It's hardcover, and not only does it have space for your everyday ramblings, but it has witty sayings and anecdotes along the margins that tie in with the writing game. It also devotes several pages to submissions so that you can keep an orderly record of what you sent and when.

I have tried to cover all kinds of noncommercial writings so that one of them will intrigue you with its possibilities. Don't wait. The sooner you become a writer, the better. The sooner you begin to communicate, the more you will have to offer the world and your inner self.

Appendix

The following is a sampling of the various kinds of writing mentioned in this book. Each one is complete instead of being an excerpt so that the beginning writer can see how a professional puts his material together. They have all been published.

These pieces range from a single line to a 900-word article. One is mine, but the others belong to those students in my classes who are determined to see their names in print. The majority of them are currently working on other literary projects.

Fillers

When Liz Gendron first joined my class, I could see that her bubbling sense of humor and witty remarks would eventually find a market. But she had a problem: she needed self-discipline in order to get her words down on paper. At first, she just sat there listening to me talk about all the different phases of writing. She's told me that it was like a field trip through history, literature, outer space, and running into Benjamin Franklin, Isaac Asimov, and Carl Sagan all on the same day. It was like finding the Ark and getting lost in the Bermuda Triangle. What she was saying, of course, was that she was hearing about all of the things I have researched and found fascinating. She finally came to the conclusion that if I could teach and do some writing, while fulfilling my familial responsibilities, so could she. And she did.

Take a good look at the following three quips. They are especially good because they spring from her thoughts as she gets into her sixties. But she's not only expressing her reactions to the aging process. She is an observer; she listens and watches people all the time. She realizes that other men and women are going through the same crises she is experiencing. She has learned from my class that there is a ready-made audience out there if she studies the market.

- I'd like to take my senior citizen's card and give it to some nice old person.
- I'm working on my senility. Every day I make it a point to forget at least one thing.

• Every time I want to go some place, my husband asks, "Is it down hill?"

(Senior Scribes, July 1980)

Al Toner is also interested in quips. He majored in English, added an M.A. from the Iowa Writers' Workshop, and wrote throughout a government career involved with foreign affairs. (It included two tours on the White House staff.) He has sold fillers to *The New Yorker* and *The Washingtonian*, and edits books and articles on international subjects. His letters to the editor on English usage in the newspaper world appear occasionally in the Washington press. He is having some success with cartoon ideas and is currently at work on sketches about growing up in Maine.

Notice that in the following quips Al Toner has given a heading to each one which adds dimension to his one-liners. He likes to cover a variety of subjects and that means he can sell to a number of markets. His embellishments make the editors sit up and take notice of his material. See for yourself from the five following examples:

- *Golden Age*
  Retirement means never having to update your resume.

- *Golden Days*
  Remember when a Saturday night special was a drugstore soda after the movie?

- *Goofy Glossary*
  Bright fish: Phi Beta Kipper.

- *Trend*
  America's changing, it's plain to see,
  From We the People, to I the Me!

- *Splice of Life*
  As future science brings new scenes,
  Will people have designer genes?

  (Senior Scribes, April 1981)

Fillers can also mean recipes. But most of the time they can only find a market if they have a story attached to them. Grace Moremen attended one of my classes several years ago and heard me expound on the fun and profit of writing for the filler market. When I told the class that I expected them to walk in the next week with some kind of tidbit, I could see she looked puzzled. But she rose to the challenge—and even brought the cake she wrote about.

Grace has written book reviews, article abstracts, and an assignment from *National Geographic.* She recently wrote a chapter for *The Women's Book of World Records and Achievements* called "Women in the Labor Movement and Organizations." She has also written a book for the preschool age group entitled *No, No, Natalie,* which tells the story (a factual account) of a rabbit walking into a nursery school and becoming a part of the scene, and a guidebook for older children when they visit Washington, D.C.

As you read this story of a recipe, notice how Grace introduces her material. She begins with an anecdote and hooks her reader immediately. Also pay attention to how she makes use of reader identification. The year was 1976, a time when we were all concerned about shortages in jobs, money, gasoline, and food. She couldn't have written a more timely filler. You'll see a postscript to this feature that Grace never expected, and one that made her story even more enjoyable.

Emergency Spice Cake

One rainy Saturday last winter while I was sifting through my envelope of loose recipes, out fell a yellowed news clipping. It was a recipe from my late grandmother's collection that I had saved because it intrigued me: a cake made without milk, eggs, or butter. Feeling caught between the pinch of shortages and the squeeze of rising food prices, I decided the moment had come for me to try this old recipe. I was hesitant about putting lard in the cake, but I needn't have been; it was undetectable. And lard is relatively cheap. Our sixteen-year-old daughter, Margie, fascinated by its lack of the usual ingredients, offered to help make it.

As it baked, our emergency cake soothed the household with a delicious spicy aroma. And later at dinner it provided my family with a surprisingly good dessert, rather like gingerbread (without any ginger). Oh yes, a bit of cheating—Margie splashed down to the corner food store and brought home some whipped topping, which we added to each piece before serving. But the leftover cake disappeared quickly even without topping as an afterschool snack on Monday.

EMERGENCY SPICE CAKE

2 cups brown or white sugar
2 cups water
2/3 cup lard
1 cup raisins
1/4 teaspoon salt (or a bit more)
1/2 teaspoon nutmeg
2 teaspoons cinnamon
1 teaspoon ground cloves
2 teaspoons baking soda mixed with 1/3 cup water
    or cold coffee
4 cups flour sifted with 1 teaspoon baking powder
1 cup chopped nuts (optional)
Whole or half nuts (optional)

Boil sugar, water, lard, raisins, salt and spices 5 minutes. Let cool, then add baking soda and flour mixtures. Mix thoroughly (batter should be quite stiff). Add chopped nuts. Pour into greased and floured rectangular or square cake pan and decorate with nuts. Bake in preheated 350° oven 30 to 35 minutes or until knife inserted in center comes out clean.

Editor's Note: One of our home economists remembered this fondly, said it was called Canada War Cake during World War I.

(*Woman's Day,* August 1976)

Another kind of filler is being written these days by Cowan McFarland, a retired Army colonel, who has recently discovered the exciting world of creative writing. Determined to get bylines as quickly as possible, he has studied the filler market and has come up with two items that appealed to the editor of a local publication. But he is also intrigued by the art of the short story and has drawn upon his background in the army to create two works of fiction, which he has sent to a new military magazine. In the meantime, Colonel McFarland is trying his hand at writing poetry.

In this first filler, it's important to point out that it was accepted because it was timely. General Omar N. Bradley had just died, and the country was paying its respects to the "soldier's soldier." Colonel McFarland decided he would send a quote of the general's to *Senior Scribes.* He had always been impressed with these words on a plaque he had purchased years ago at Freedom Foundation, Valley Forge, Pennsylvania, and now was the time to share it with other Americans. It read:

> Freedom—no word was ever spoken that has held out greater hope, demanded greater sacrifice, needed more to be nurtured, blessed more the giver, damned more its destroyer, or came closer to being God's will on earth. May America ever be its protector!

In his second filler, he tells his readers what happens when he goes walking along country roads and city streets:

On my daily walks I see many fascinating, eye-catching sights, items, and activities. Recently, I noted three timely, provocative bumper stickers: Make Today Count: One Step at a Time; and Keep Going. Noting these, I added a new zest to my step and was prompted to blend them into my daily philosophy of living. Such discoveries prove too that you can be pleasantly surprised and positively motivated by just taking a walk.

(*Senior Scribes*, April 1981)

I'd like to add an important footnote here: This writer keeps a journal in which he writes almost every day.

The following poem also comes under the heading of a filler. It was written by Mary Ann Lundy, the wife of a foreign service officer who had accompanied her husband on a number of overseas assignments. During a recent Washington tour, she signed up for one of my classes in creative writing. I later learned that she had wanted to write even as a child. But through the years of moving and taking care of her family, there never seemed to be enough time. One day, she decided the time had come to fulfill a lifelong ambition.

I'd like to point out that Mary Ann believed in studying her markets. When she read several copies of *The Kindergartner*, published by the United Methodist Church, she was almost sure that her poem would find a home there. You may also be interested in knowing that the idea for the poem came from a visit to the home of Mary Ann's parents. While there, her son took her around the house and pointed out various things which had mysteriously grown "smaller" over the years. Here are the lines she wrote:

Changing

Each time I go to Grandma's house,
The things all seem so small.

Did I really do three somersaults
In her little narrow hall?

That space behind my Grandad's desk
Where I can barely peek.

I can't believe I crawled in there
For games of hide and seek!

The light switch in the kitchen,
So high up on the wall,

Why, I can turn it off and on
And not reach up at all!

These things seem so much smaller
And different now, it's true,

But Grandma laughs and tells me
That she thinks I'm changing too!

A filler that can find a ready market on the adult or juvenile level is the puzzle. If you have a flair for this kind of writing, cultivate it. I wrote this puzzle for the reluctant reader in junior high school; I knew I'd have to make it unique in order to catch his attention. It was bought by an educational publisher in Michigan who is hoping I will do some other work for him.

You, too, can sell some material in this category. But you will have to train yourself to be on the lookout for unusual facts as you do your reading. And this is when your scribbled notes in that little notebook can pay off. Plan now to get into the habit of jotting down items that can earn you some money or a byline. And now take a look at the following:

See how many three- and four-letter words you can find in the following puzzle. You are allowed to go across and back and up and down. You should be able to spot at least 30 words in this special group of letters.

```
L O P A D O T E N A C H O S O L A C H O
G A L L O K R A N I O L E I P S A N O D
R I M H Y G U T R I M M A T O S I L P H
I O P A R A O M E I T O K A T A K E C H
Y M E N O K I C H L E P I K O S S Y P H
O P H A T T O P E R I S G E R A L E K T
R Y O N O P T E K E P H A L L I O K G K
L O P E L E I O L A G O I O S I R A I O
B A P H E T R A G A N O P T E R Y G O N
O N
```

If you are wondering why the last line has only two letters, this is not an ordinary kind of puzzle. It is actually the longest word ever to appear in literature. It contains 182 letters. It was used by Aristophanes, a Greek writer who lived more than 2300 years ago. What does it mean? It describes a stew or goulash made from fourteen-day leftovers.

(Christopher Lee Publishers)

This next filler may not bring in any money, but it will give you a byline. When Helen Bachmann was a member of my class last year, she wasn't sure what kind of writing she preferred. In fact, she had a feeling that writing was beyond her ken because it was brand-new to her. Then one day she came in and said that something had to be done about getting a bus for the senior citizens in Arlington. She was going to do something about it. Several months later, I came across her letter to the editor in the *Arlington Journal.*

As you read it, you can see that Helen said succinctly what was wrong and what had to be done. She did her homework by checking facts and statistics so that her letter would have more clout. This is the first time she has seen her name in print, but I'm sure it won't be the last. Did they get the bus? Yes, they did. Even letters to the editor can start a beginning writer on the road to successful writing.

Editor, the *Journal:*

Arlington County is home to 26,000 senior citizens. There are 4,000 of us very active in the wonderful programs Arlington County Recreation Department has for us. The big problem is that we desperately need a bus of our own.

There are only 15,000 school students who are served by 61 school buses. We are glad they have them and can go on field trips and sports events, etc.

We are only asking that we have one bus to take day trips. We pay for a portion of the cost toward the maintenance of a vehicle. We have had a discarded school bus for the past seven years. It has broken down on trips and has been out of service for repairs for as many as seven weeks at a time. We have a rhythm band that visits hospitals and nursing homes to entertain residents there. It needs a bus.

Won't someone help us convince the Arlington County Board to provide us with a bus?

Helen M. Bachmann
Arlington

Short Features

Do you have a hobby? Wade Fleetwood wrote about his sand collecting and sold it to the *National Observer.* Wade is a government employee who has traveled to many countries. He didn't think of this hobby until he was in the east coast port of Limon in Costa Rica. He tells the story that he was fascinated by the fine-grained black sand which looked like gunpowder. He was even more intrigued when he traveled to the west coast and found that the sand was brown. From then on, he began to collect grains of sand from all over the world. He also writes columns for two weekly newspapers that cater to readers who spend their vacations at the beach, and is designing brochures and travel guides for coastal businessmen.

When you read this feature, notice how Wade uses specifics

whenever he can. He describes the various shades of sand in such a way that we'll never again take for granted that all seashores are a light tan color. And even though this is a short feature, he has followed the guidelines of good article writing by introducing his subject with a narrative hook (how many people collect sand?) and wrapping it up with a summary ending.

Yeah, I collect sand. I guess it all started on my last trip to Costa Rica.

While in the east-coast port of Limon, I was fascinated by the extremely fine-grained black sand, which looked just like gunpowder. Then, traveling to the beach area at Puntarenas, on Costa Rica's west coast, I found that the sand was brown! Using 35mm cans to bring my samples home, I decided to start a sand collection.

I'm sure that I'm not the original sandman. But I dare say that I may have the only sand collection on the Virginia and Maryland coasts. Maybe throw in Delaware and North Carolina. The collection now consists of samples from Europe, Asia, Africa, and Latin America, representing some fifteen or twenty countries, together with sand from all sections of the United States.

And it just keeps sifting in. People have brought me sand from places they have visited. And people send it to me. Just the other day I received in the mail a package of sand from Corregidor Island in the Philippines. A friend brought me a cigar tube full of sand from an island in the Gulf of Siam. My daughter remembered to bring me some sand from Myrtle Beach, S.C., on a vacation. In my travels, I have scooped up sample grains from Repulse Bay in Hong Kong, as well as from the Mississippi at New Orleans, from San Francisco, from the Oregon coast, from the beaches up and down the East Coast.

I have sort of a standard ritual to prepare sand for display. If it arrives wet or damp from the container, I spread it out on a plate in the sun to dry. It is then poured, ever so carefully, into a glass cigar tube, capped, labeled and placed in a display rack.

I guess the real intrigue of it to me is that sand is not just sand. Of the samples I now have, none is like any other. Even samples from a 10-mile stretch of the same beach are different.

Now, while I could call in a technician to scientifically describe for you some of this sand, I decided that, as a layman, I could tell you what it looks like to me. Here are a few of my observations:

The sand from Bermuda is pink. Really! And very fine. And the sand from Pensacola, Fla., is like salt. Very white. From Portugal, my sample is quite coarse and multicolored, while that from Niger in the African Sahara is light brown and of face-powder texture. The Corregidor sand is like salt and pepper, coarse-ground. New Orleans' sand is white (called "sugar sand" by locals), while its river sand is yellow. Seaside Oregon sand has the black, volcanic look. In Key West the sand is similar to my sample from the Gulf of Siam; both have a coral composition. The finest and whitest sand in my collection is from St. Petersburg, Fla.

While over the years I've collected bottle caps, bird eggs, stamps, tinfoil, coins, and brass, I'm sort of caught up in the nitty-gritty of sand.

(*National Observer*, October 9, 1976)

A number of my students have written short features for magazines and newspapers at the local and national level. Lois Miller was pleasantly surprised when she was able to sell a tribute to her father to *Seek*, a religious publication, a short time after signing up for my "Write Now!" class. While she maintains that I was responsible for her quick success, I honestly believe that it happened because she followed the guidelines and wrote from the heart. She has also sold a religious article to *Living with Children*, and plans to write some children's stories and a gothic this year.

Lois sold her article because the editors knew that her problem would find reader identification. She wrote her account of her divorce in a straightforward fashion and in such a way that it would help other women live through such an ordeal. Here is her story:

Several years ago my seventeen-year marriage came to a shattering halt. I was totally unprepared for it. I believe in marriage "till death do us part," but found myself facing a separation, and finally a divorce. I was in the depths of despair, and also very frightened.

How could I manage to raise my two boys, ages 11 and 15? I wanted the best for my sons, and wasn't thinking as much about material things as I was about the ideals I wanted them to learn.

My wish for my sons was for them to grow up to be fine responsible men who cared about other people. Could this be done alone? I could *not* do it alone. I asked God to help me, and I knew I couldn't just sit back and feel sorry for myself. I had to do my part. I had to try to help myself with my future life. Then God would help.

I knew I should try to find a job. I was more fortunate than a lot of women in this position. I had financial security from my ex-husband. I felt I should try to find employment, though, to hedge against unexpected expenses and—well, I didn't know what the future held.

The prospect of a job interview terrified me. I had married after only two years of college, and I had no job experience.

One year of typing in high school didn't give me much marketable skill. A refresher course at the Y.W.C.A. helped.

I had always been a shy person without much confidence. Now, my ego had been shattered. I wanted to give up on everything, but deep down I knew I had to somehow pick up the pieces and begin a new life.

A friend of my next-door neighbor gave me a pep talk before I left for my first job interview. He told me I could do it. He saw how frightened I was, and tried to give me some confidence. It helped a lot. I prayed all the way to the interview. I kept repeating silently the Bible verse, "Fear thou not; for I am with thee; be not dismayed; for I am thy God; I will strengthen thee" (Isaiah 4:10). I got the job. It was a part-time job and didn't pay much, but it was a start.

I found out that I could do the work satisfactorily. I also made many friends. I became more sensitive to other people's problems, because of my own experience. It was easier to talk to them because I had "been there." I was more aware of their feelings, and felt I could give them some hope.

This was a learning time in my life: learning new skills and learning how to cope with problems and situations as they came. Many times I was at my wit's end, but I asked God to give me the strength to do all the things I had to do. I also asked for wisdom to deal with problems as they arose.

My dad was a big help. He has a great philosophy of life. He has overcome many problems and has managed to maintain a healthy attitude. Dad always told me there are two ways of looking at life. We can be sad because of what we don't have, or we can be thankful for what we *do* have. This is what makes a person happy or unhappy. It depends upon one's perspective.

When problems already had brought me down to what seemed the breaking point, Dad had a heart attack. I didn't know if he would pull through. It was a severe attack, and he was in the hospital a month. I am thankful God spared him. I really needed him.

I had much for which to be thankful. Dad's life had been spared. Mother and Dad had been such a help to me. My friends and relatives were loving and kind. I had made some friendships I will always treasure. I had two fine sons. There were many obstacles to overcome along the way, but I had God's help.

After several steps up the job ladder, I started working full-time. I found I was gaining confidence and I could relate to people with problems.

I came out of the whole experience much stronger. I am more sensitive and compassionate. I can always listen.

Something else wonderful has happened. A man I had known only slightly before has now become very important in my life. (He was the one who gave me encouragement before my first job interview.) We later started dating. We developed a relationship I never thought possible. He is sympathetic, kind, and understanding. We seem to know each other's thoughts without saying a word.

In a few years we were married. It was the happiest day of my life. My youngest son, who was sixteen years of age at the time, was in the wedding party. My oldest son, who was in the Navy, called me from Guam at 6:00 in the morning the day of the wedding. He wanted to wish me every happiness.

Like Dad told me: "This world that we're a livin' in is mighty hard to beat; you get a thorn with every rose, but ain't the roses sweet?"

(*Seek*, October 12, 1980)

When librarian Mildred Askegaard decided to retire in 1975 and do some traveling, she also made up her mind to learn how to write articles and stories. That was the year that she walked into one of my classes determined to go on trips and then write about them. I was more than pleased when she returned from a jaunt to Alaska and handed me the following account of her experiences there. It was published in the *Arlington News*.

I especially liked some of her light touches; travel articles can be deadly with their descriptions of places to visit or things to see if they aren't lightened with some humor or fascinating tidbits. When you read her feature, you'll see she has used a kind of you-are-there technique that makes the reader feel that he is on the trip with her. Her first line delighted me with its breezy introduction to that awesome state with its many glaciers and snowcapped mountains.

There I was, sitting on a log, eating Glacier Goulash, looking at one of the wonders of the world, 20,300-foot snow-

capped Mt. McKinley, the loftiest peak in North America. For this experience, I had traveled 3,464 air miles, eight hours by train, and another eight on a bus. Our viewing spot, Stoney Hill, on the 87-mile road inside the Park, was 20 miles from the base and 35 miles from the peak of the mountain. Fog, rain, snow, and clouds often prevent a good view of the mountain, so we felt particularly fortunate that the sun came out in time for us to get this fascinating look at McKinley. Surrounding snow-peaked mountains of the Alaska Range added to the beauty of the scene.

Another feature of the Park is the wildlife. Private cars are not allowed on the Denali road except to go to the camp-ground, so we boarded a bus for the wildlife tour. I soon discovered—along with the rest of the passengers—that no one is allowed out of the bus except at designated places and that the rule is enforced to protect the wild animals. I also learned that each rest stop is checked by the guide to make sure a shaggy bear isn't lurking in the rest room!

Along the route, we saw a bull and a cow moose feeding in the brush; a good view of grizzlies tackling some kind of small game; and a lone caribou grazing with two bulls fighting not too far away. As we crossed a glacial river, golden eagles swooped and soared on the air currents. Ptarmigan, in its brownish, bared summer plumage, was quietly hiding in the brush. The white Dall sheep grazed high on a distant moun-tain.

The Indians called the towering Mt. McKinley "Denali, the Great One." The name was changed in 1897 in honor of the new president, William McKinley. There is now a move to change the name back to "Denali."

At the end of the summer, the Alaska railroad reduces its trips from Anchorage to Fairbanks from daily to three times a week. The lodge closes and before long the snows come and cover the area. Denali Road closes off and the only sound consists of the cross-country skiers and the sled dogs making their patrol rounds. But that is all as it should be: the Park, the wildlife and the mountains should be allowed to rejuvenate before the onslaught of the summer of '76.

(*Arlington News*, November 6, 1975)

Feature writing has always appealed to Nan Carroll, a former army wife who lives in Arlington. A few years ago, she did a "Landmark" series for the *Washington Post* in which she described certain places in the area, always adding a bit of information that surprised the reader and made him want to know more. Nan worked for the *Ladies Home Journal* in her salad days, and wrote a book during the Bicentennial year called *Gentlemen of Virginia*. Her great interest in research has led to many a sale, particularly with stories about the Civil War.

In this feature on Bailey's Crossroads, a nearby town, she did interviews and made phone calls in addition to reading all kinds of books and old newspapers. As you read this "Landscape" you can see why the editors decided to buy it.

Busy shops, banks, apartments, and traffic today congest Bailey's Crossroads ... where once elephants were quartered and the whip-crack of lion trainers echoed through a quiet countryside.

More than 500 acres in Fairfax county were purchased in December 1837 by Hachaliah Bailey of New York who needed a country place near the Washington, D.C., area for training and wintering a collection of animals he exhibited summers in traveling road show circuses.

Six years later, "Hack" Bailey deeded the property to 36-year-old Mariah, wife of his son Lewis, who with their ten children lived there in a mansion named "Maury." ("Maury" was reputed to have had 100 rooms.) At the crossroads of Columbia turnpike and Leesburg turnpike Lewis and Mariah Bailey managed a long, rambling tavern-type inn which accommodated circus personnel, travelers, and drovers en route to Washington market.

Although Lewis raised crops and cattle, he never considered himself a farmer, but raised only what was needed for the inn and the circus clientele.

When the circus was in winter quarters the quiet Virginia countryside resounded with weird shrieks, growls, and screeches. Besides the work and show horses quartered there were elephants, camels, zebras, giraffes, monkeys, dogs, lions, tigers, and an occasional hippopotamus which, when traveling, required the wagon-pulling power of fourteen horses. Bailey's Crossroads became a free winter circus for neighbors and passersby.

The circus was eagerly anticipated in those days and included, besides clowns, an impressive collection of wild animals and trick horseback riders. One show with which the Baileys were closely associated was the Aaron Turner Circus. This was the first circus to use a canvas tent to shelter the show and spectators. George F. Bailey, Hack's nephew, was married to the daughter of Aaron Turner and managed the circus on tours throughout the South, Cuba, and South America.

During these years a young man Hack Bailey had hired in New York in the 1820s frequently traveled with Turner Circus; his name was Phineas T. Barnum.

In 1875, thirty years after the death of Hack Bailey, P.T. Barnum bought a circus owned by George F. Bailey. Six years later he merged his show with a circus assembled by a young orphan, James McGinnis, who had run away to join the circus. Perhaps because of the interest shown in the orphan by Fred Bailey, Mariah's brother-in-law, young James took the name "Bailey." With the merger in 1881 Barnum first proclaimed "The Greatest Show on Earth."

Several years later the circus moved its winter quarters to Sarasota, Florida.

Bailey's Crossroads in Fairfax county bears the name of the man P.T. Barnum called in his autobiography "The father of the American circus."

(Arlington News, April 24, 1970)

When Ruth Woodside took one of my writing classes, I encouraged her to write material that would put her scientific background to good use. She had been a biology teacher for years, and wanted to tell the layman what a wonderful world existed out there if he would only become aware of it. She is now beginning to do that very thing and plans to write about nutrition and health issues as time goes on.

At the present time, she is writing material for *Senior Scribes*, and is proud of her first byline on the following feature on autumn leaves. Without any prompting, she started her lead or narrative hook with a quote which tied in with the subject she planned to discuss. She was careful not to sound as though she were giving a lecture in a class in botany.

> Ladies at a ball
> Are not as fine as these
> Richly brocaded trees
> That decorate the fall.
> —Jean Starr Untermeyer

It seems as if Cinderella's fairy godmother waves her wand and the colors of autumn appear. The greens of spring and summer are transformed into a profusion of yellows, reds, oranges. This phenomenon occurs in middle latitudes where there is enough precipitation to support broad-leaved trees.

But what really happens inside the plant to cause these brilliant colors?

In the fall when the weather is cooler and the hours of daylight are less, a layer of thin-walled cells forms where the leaf-stalk joins the stem or branch.

The food-manufacturing structures in a leaf are the chloroplasts. These contain three pigments: green, yellow, yellow-orange. The green pigment or chlorophyll is unstable and has to be constantly replaced, but due to the buildup of this special layer, necessary substances are unable to pass into the leaf. When the chlorophyll disappears, the already present yellows and yellow-oranges are unmasked.

Red-blue pigments are formed in the cell sap outside the chloroplast from sugars and wastes trapped in the leaf. If there is a sudden drop in temperature, flaming reds develop. Eventually the cells die. The leaf turns brown and drops from the tree. Deciduous trees are dormant during the winter. In the spring new leaves develop and the cycle continues.

Articles

Dody Smith wrote the following article when eight of us hunted for gold in Centreville after reading a newspaper account that it had never been found after General Braddock's defeat in 1755 during the French and Indian War. (I describe the outing in Chapter 2.) After our fruitless search, I decided that my would-be writers should write up in detail what happened that day in May when we packed a picnic lunch and stepped back in time to the eighteenth century. I told them that it would be a contest and that the winner would be chosen by the editor of the *Arlington News*, who would be gracious enough to publish it. And all of that came to pass. Dody won the contest, but I must admit there were several others that were a close second.

Dody Smith served as communications watch officer in the U.S. Navy's Women Accepted for Volunteer Emergency Service (WAVES) from 1943 to 1946, and is married to a retired navy captain. This story about the hunt for gold was her first attempt to put an article together. Since that time, she has written occasionally for the *Washington Post*, the *Baltimore Sun*, and *Naval Institute Proceedings*. She has also contributed material to *The People's Almanac*.

When you read the following lighthearted article, take a second look at the dialogue. Dody's retentive memory picked up all kinds of lines we spoke to each other in class and on our prospecting adventure. Nan Carroll at the time was searching for information on Antonia Ford, a Confederate spy, and the rest of us were still trying to solve the mystery of the disappearance of Donna, an attractive redhead and promising young writer. (When I called her home, I was told that no one lived there by that name.) Now that I have filled you in on some of the hidden meanings in the remarks that were made, enjoy Dody's article. Do notice how it seems to flow from paragraph to paragraph.

A latter-day gold rush was the final session for Peggy Teeters' "Write Now" class on May 20. Her indomitable group of aspiring writers, having writ, moved on to Centreville in search of Braddock's gold.

"Who was Braddock? What gold?" you might ask (as many of the class did).

Well, it all started when someone produced an old news clipping about the legend that persists concerning Major General Braddock of the British Army and his ill-fated expedition against Fort Duquesne during the French and Indian War, 1755. According to this story, General Braddock was leading a division of Virginia riflemen and six companies of the 44th British Regiment, including artillery and baggage wagons, from Alexandria toward Winchester, when the going got so rough through the mud and forests, they had to lighten the load. Soldiers were ordered to dismount two brass cannons, fill their muzzles with $25,000 in gold coin (the troop's payroll), and bury them. Thus unburdened, the troops pressed onward—unfortunately into their disastrous ambush. General Braddock and all the men who knew where the gold was buried were killed. Braddock's reports and papers were later sent to England and filed away. Supposedly an archivist came upon the report of the buried payroll many years later.

A committee was formed in England and sent to Centreville to search for it. The gold was never found. Or at least that's the way the story goes.

At Wilson Elementary School, where the Adult Education "Write Now" classes met, corridors echoed that day with cacophonous points and counterpoints:

"It can't be there NOW."

"How do you know?"

"Maybe somebody found it and just kept quiet."

"What if they didn't?"

"Are you sure Braddock passed near Centreville?"

"Didn't he cross the Potomac at Antonia Ford?"

"You're mixed up. That's not a place."

"What happened to Donna?"

"It would be a great scoop if we found the gold."

"Wouldn't we have to give it back to the British?"

"They say we could have half."

Gaveling the group to order, Teacher Teeters suggested that a fitting climax to fruitful class sessions such as this group has experienced would be to have a picnic. Why not select a site near the legendary treasure spot and keep an alert eye just in case a cannon muzzle may be sticking up somewhere?

Again the class members responded enthusiastically:

"I'll bring the fruit."

"Who is good at reading maps?"

"Can somebody bring a metal detector?"

"Yes, but it works only to a depth of five inches."

"That's fine—my garden spade goes about that deep."

So a committee was formed in Arlington and sent to Centreville. But history indeed repeats itself. The gold was never found.

What was found, however, was a rare thing for this group—a unanimous decision. Every member of the expedition quickly agreed that this was a wonderful idea for a picnic.

Several years ago, Muriel McKenna retired after twenty years' service as a librarian with the Veterans Administration and soon came to one big conclusion: there had to be some kind of creative activity in her life. So she dusted off her little electric typewriter and began to write a book. She had always been interested in solo performers in the theater. She decided to do some research and work on one chapter at a time. Eventually, she sold her story about Ruth Draper to Crown, who published it in an anthology called

Women in the American Theater. A short version is also in the new volume of *Notable American Women* published by Harvard. But as she works on her chapters, she is also doing other kinds of writing. You'll see that her research abilities are outstanding as you read her article about a beetle. It found a home in the *Arlington News* and encouraged her to do some more writing in this category. At the present time, she is trying her hand at children's stories and poetry.

When you read this article, you'll see that Muriel has read many a book on ancient Egypt in order to make her material appealing. But also note that she tells an anecdote or two and uses a quote; both of these techniques liven up her information on this insect. Her last paragraph is especially effective because it ties in the ancient beetle with today's world.

In ancient Egypt the Egyptians worshiped, of all things, a beetle. It was called a scarab later, from the Latin name for it, *scarabacus.* The particular beetle portrayed so much in Egyptian artifacts is the so-called dung beetle.

The dung beetle found around the Nile is an almost circular little creature, about two and one half inches long, with a tint of gold. It has a most peculiar habit, which gives it its name and also indirectly explains why the Egyptians considered it as a symbol of one of their gods.

On sunny days the little insect pushes tiny balls of dung along to its nest, apparently laying its eggs in the ball. Soon the banks of the Nile are teeming with new scarabs. This led the Egyptians to believe that they appeared by spontaneous generation.

The little beetle, pushing its tiny ball along, reminded the Egyptians of the sun god above, who they believed pushed the great ball of sun across the sky every day. So the scarab, the little dung beetle, became the symbol of the sun god, the personification of the Sun God Ra or Khebra. He seemed also a symbol of immortality.

We find the earliest artifacts in the form of a scarab in the late Old Kingdom of Egyptian history (c. 2686-2160 B.C.). Some were merely amulets or charms, some merely ornaments, others may have been used as seals.

From the New Kingdom (1567-1085 B.C.) and later, the scarab was a very important part of the elaborate burial rites of the period, especially for royalty. It was believed that after death one's soul was brought to judgment before Osiris, god of the Underworld. Many amulets and other treasures were placed in the mummy shroud to help the deceased at that time. Most important was the "heart scarab," a large charm in the form of a scarab that was placed over the heart. Usually there was an inscription on the underside begging the heart not to inform against the deceased at the time of judgment.

Many different materials were used to make the scarab amulets and seals—basalt, glazed pottery, various precious and semiprecious stones (except, perhaps diamonds, opals, rubies and sapphires, which were not known at that time and place). The smooth base underneath was usually inscribed with lucky symbols, hieroglyphics, or other sayings, and there were special ceremonies at which they were blessed when the astrologer said it was propitious.

Some of the inscriptions found on amulets of the Middle Kingdom period (2065-1580 B.C.) include titles of officials and other designs. Later some of the seals were inscribed with mottoes, references to places or to some gods, or merely with good luck signs.

The most valuable ones, of course, had royal names and more distinctive patterns or designs. King Amenhotep III issued a series of commemorative seals to inform his people of his marriage to a commoner in the following words: "May he live, Amenhotep, given life, and the King's great wife Ti, who lives. The name of her father is Yuya, the name of her mother is Tuya, she is the wife of the mighty king, whose southern boundary is as far as Karoy, and northern as far as Naharini." Apparently he wanted to assure that Ti received the proper respect to which she was entitled as his queen.

Scarab amulets and seals were imitated all over the Mediterranean world as the centuries passed. Romans made them into signet rings, usually on a swivel so that they could be worn as a necklace.

Even today the scarab is very popular as a motif in jewelry design, if no longer an object of worship. One can find many inexpensive tourist souvenirs almost everywhere, and also some very lovely, expensive pieces of jewelry in precious and semiprecious stones made into rings, bracelets, pendants, earrings and necklaces. You don't have to travel to Egypt to find them, either.

I'll always remember the day Earle Sawyer came into my class at Culpepper Garden. Tall, slender, ramrod straight, he typified the "gentleman from the old school." And that he was—in more ways than one. He had very definite opinions on almost everything. When I tried to tell him that he could learn how to write a filler, do an article, and create a piece of fiction, he was sure he couldn't. Everything he wrote promptly came back. Surely his ten years in the Philippines as a teacher should be a source for many good articles and stories! I agreed with him and asked him to read some of his rejections to the class. With some constructive criticism (offered in a gingerly fashion), Earle finally realized that there are some rules which should be followed. Several months later, he sold four fillers and the following article to the *Navy News*. The "gentleman from the old school" is beaming these days.

I'd like to point out that the lead of Earle's article is simple but so effective in announcing that Commodore Dewey destroyed the Spanish Asiatic Squadron before lunch. Notice how he adds a quote here and there so that the article isn't all straight narrative. He also managed to find some photos for his story. But I'm pleased most of all with Earle's willingness to make changes in his manuscript before mailing it out again. You might like to know that this author is now in his eighties.

Commodore George E. Dewey, U.S.N., destroyed the

Spanish Asiatic Squadron before lunch on May 1st, 1898.

On August 13th Commodore Dewey's forces, acting in coordination with the Army forces under the command of General Wesley Merritt, required about the same length of time to take Manila.

The victory of cooperating Army and Navy forces operating in Manila Bay on that August morning, to some extent, set the pattern for the joining of American Army and Navy forces to capture Manila from the Japanese on an August morning in 1945.

On January 8, 1898, Commodore George E. Dewey was placed in command of the American Asiatic Squadron, which at that moment was in Nagasaki, Japan.

By February 25th, when the Assistant Secretary of the Navy, Theodore Roosevelt, ordered Commodore Dewey to take his squadron to Hong Kong, Dewey, chagrined because he had not been promoted to Rear Admiral, had used every available opportunity to complete his extensive studies of the Orient.

The Navy instructed the Commodore to prepare his squadron for action against the Spanish squadron in the event war was declared between the United States and Spain. The order was also stipulated that he, Dewey, was to be certain he had sufficient coal, and retain the Olympia pending further orders.

Dewey's first action at Hong Kong was to have his ships drydocked, scraped, and painted.

To further strengthen his squadron he purchased the British collier Nashan, and the merchantman Zafiro. Then he took on all of the coal and ammunition for which there was space.

Believing the squadron would be safer, and less noticeable in the small bay, Mirs, which was adjacent to Hong Kong, he moved it there.

In further preparation for the battle he was certain he would have, he threw all wood, all combustible materials, and all property of the crew that could be spared overboard.

While the Commodore was busily preparing his forces for entrance into Manila Bay he was being constantly annoyed by a small group of Filipino patriots who were anxious to get Dewey to commit himself to independence for the Philippines in the event of victory.

Sometime after his victory in Manila Bay, and his return to the United States Dewey explained to a Senate committee regarding these patriots, "I did not attach the slightest importance to anything they could do, and they did nothing ... finally I would not see them at all, but turned them over to my staff."

The orders Commodore Dewey received from the Secretary of the Navy on April 25th ended all bickering between Dewey and the insurgents. The order stated that war had been declared between the United States and Spain. Offensive operations against the Spanish squadron were to begin immediately. "You must capture vessels, or destroy. Use utmost endeavors."

At this time Dewey was undoubtedly anxious to get started for Manila. However, to further assure victory he took two days for target practice with the eight-inch rifles, firing them point blank into the hills around the bay. He even found time for torpedo practice.

On April 27th, Dewey, knowing his squadron was ready, sailed from Mirs Bay into the South China Sea shortly after noon. Crew morale was at its highest possible peak. Everyone aboard was sure of victory.

By midnight on May 1st the American Squadron stood off Manila Bay. There were two entrances into the bay, and the Commodore knew both had been mined by the Spaniards. The reason for taking his chances with the one he selected was not guess work. He knew the Spaniards were still quite ignorant on the subject of mine laying, especially in deep water. Therefore, he decided on the deeper channel.

Another, more serious problem was the Spanish shore guns. These could alter the outcome of the engagement, since almost every square foot of the bay was under one or another of these batteries.

Other possibilities for defeat lay in the fact his coal ships had to be properly deployed as their loss would make victory impossible. Furthermore, there were no repair facilities available should one or more of his fighting ships be hit hard, and thus disabled.

Without hesitation Dewey sailed his squadron into Manila Bay. By four o'clock all of the ships were in the bay. Enroute, one defensive shore battery, located on an island near the entrance to the bay fired upon them. Dewey's return fire quickly silenced that battery.

Dewey, once the whole squadron was in the bay, instructed his navigator, "Mr. Calkins, take her close along the five-fathom line, but be careful not to get her aground."

At 5:41 a.m. he said from the bridge, "You may fire when you are ready, Gridley."

From 5:45 to 7:35, when Dewey withdrew because of a false report about ammunition shortages, Dewey's ships passed up and down the Spanish line, wreaking havoc among Admiral Montojo's squadron. After another hour of destruction, from 11 to noon, all of Montojo's ships were burned, sunk or abandoned. The Spanish suffered 381 killed or wounded; Dewey's losses were seven wounded, none killed. Dewey's 170 hits on the Spanish sharply contrasted with the Spanish total of 15 on the American ships. Dewey's preparation was the key to his victory; as Dewey said, "The battle of Manila was won in Hong Kong harbor."

Seven Spanish fighting ships had been sunk, and three supply ships captured.

Dewey controlled the bay completely until August 13th when he and General Wesley Merritt joined forces to capture Manila.

It was almost a year before Dewey was ordered home. There he received a hero's welcome, due the rank of Admiral of the Navy with life tenure.

Nostalgia

Florence McConnell was born in 1887 in Mayville, New York. She attended Fredonia Normal School and taught for several years before her marriage in 1916. She had three children and lived for many years in northern New Jersey where her husband taught agriculture. She returned to teaching as a substitute at an age when most teachers retire. In her late eighties, a widow, she came to Culpepper Garden, where she began to write about family history and her younger years.

She wrote the following story when she was ninety-two. It made quite an impression on the members of the class as she read it aloud. If you are planning to write some nostalgia about your childhood, this short feature should help you recall those early days.

Memories of childhood in the small village of Mayville, New York, include living before modern conveniences like a furnace and electricity were a part of one's home or town. Our heat was by a large coal stove in the sitting room with squares of isinglass insets showing the glowing bed of coals. Our kitchen stove burned either coal or wood for cooking and baking and had a large space attached for heating water.

I still remember the corner in the sitting room behind the coal stove where I used to dress on those wintry mornings. Our dog, Frank, a big, white friendly animal with a black spot here and there, enjoyed that corner also. In fact, this was the rallying place for the whole family during those winter days.

As I grew up, Frank followed me many times as I was delivering pails of milk to the neighbors on my bicycle. My father, even though he was Clerk of the Surrogate for the county of Chautauqua with its two cities of Jamestown and Dunkirk, always kept a horse and one or two cows which he cared for. He believed this gave him needed exercise. So our barn always had a big hayloft where Frank, the dog, slept at night (he preferred, of course, to stay inside).

Even though I am now in my nineties, I can still recall one incident involving Frank from the dim and distant past. We were spending the evening, as usual, around the stove in the sitting room. Frank was also there, in the corner near the stove. The conversation happened to center around the fact that old Frank was showing his age, and we wondered, as we talked, if he would be around much longer. We also discussed methods of disposal.

At bedtime, Father took Frank to the barn for him to sleep in the hay. When he let him out in the morning, he went on with his chores; little did he think that Frank had disappeared never to be seen again. We searched everywhere that day, even behind the big snowdrifts, but there was no sign of Frank.

In the spring, when two neighbors were gathering cowslips in the swamp way outside of town, there they found the body of old Frank. He demonstrated to us with a certainty that he had comprehended all we said in our discussion of how to put him away—and had taken upon himself the solution of the problem.

Inez Whitney's feature on her mother's oatmeal cookies takes us on a delightful trip to the days of her childhood, and also shares with us a recipe that is something special. Inez grew up in Custer, Oklahoma, and became a teacher of primary grades in Oklahoma City. During those years, she developed an interest in creative writing, and knew that some day she would put her thoughts down on paper. She now meets once a week with other writers at the historic farmhouse in Falls Church, Virginia, that once belonged to the aunt and uncle of James Whitcomb Riley. Inez is finally turning out a variety of articles on travel and nostalgia; the ghost of the famous poet seems to be exerting an influence in the right direction.

If cooking is your forte, take a look at the way in which Inez presents this cookie recipe. The story she tells about it makes it so much more than a list of ingredients. She describes how it has been handed down through the generations of her family. She also talks about baking them for her own children and grandchildren, and mentions that even her friends are enjoying these delectable morsels with no regard for the calories. I can vouch for that.

Ever since I can remember, Mama's oatmeal cookies were my favorite. How happy I was to come home from school and find stacks of them on the kitchen table just out of the oven. I could smell them the minute I came into the house.

When my Aunt Gertie came over with my cousins, Mama always made sure to have some in a dish on the dining room table. How well I remember that dish—a beautiful, large, pressed glass compote with a lid. And when we kids tried to steal a cookie, the clank of that metal lid always gave us away.

Mama told me one day how she happened to have the recipe. She said, "Your Aunt Mettie made a trip back to Indiana for her mother and father's fiftieth wedding anniversary. All the children, grandchildren, great-grandchildren, and dozens of relatives came. The year was 1910 and everyone was amazed that Mettie and her little girls had made the long journey from Oklahoma. There was a formal wedding at the church for the renewal of marriage vows. When the couple reached home, a grandson carried the bride across the threshold.

"Inside the tables were loaded with all kinds of food. Every lady had brought her favorite dish. Mettie said she heard someone whisper: 'Look at that plate of oatmeal cookies Sarah brought! Wouldn't you think she could have made something a little bit fancier?' But in a short while the oatmeal cookies had disappeared, and everyone was asking for the recipe."

Aunt Mettie brought the recipe back to Oklahoma and gave it to my mother.

I have made these cookies for my son, daughter, grandchildren, and now great-grandchildren. When my daughter Linda had little girls of her own, she said, "Mother, I want to be sure to get that oatmeal cookie recipe. The kids want me to make some."

I have given it to many relatives and friends and now I'll share it with you.

Mama's Oatmeal Cookies
3 cups sugar
2 cups shortening
7 eggs
2 cups flour
1 teaspoon salt
1 teaspoon soda
1 teaspoon baking powder
6 cups oatmeal (old-fashioned. Don't use Minute Oats)
½ lb raisins

Cream sugar and shortening. Add eggs. Then add flour sifted with salt, soda and baking powder. Up to this point an electric mixer can be used. Then fold in raisins and oatmeal by hand. Drop by rounded teaspoons on a greased cookie sheet. Bake about 8-10 minutes in a 350-degree oven. They will raise, flatten out, and be only very lightly browned when they are done. Remove from the cookie sheet at once. I usually make only half of the recipe, which makes about 7 dozen. Use either 3 large, or 4 small eggs. Raisins can be omitted.

Suggested Reading

Bray, Jean A. "Writing About the Past for the Present," *The Writer*, January, 1980. Here are some tips for nostalgia buffs who are looking for ideas that will find a receptive market in the 1980s.

Burack, A. S. *How to Write Fillers That Sell*, Boston: The Writer, 1977. You'll learn how to market your filler whether it's informative, entertaining, or unusual. You'll also discover that your choice of subject plays an important role in this field.

————. *The Writer's Handbook*, Boston: The Writer, 1986. This book is a complete guide to all aspects of freelance writing. In it, 100 experts give advice ranging from how to sell light verse to the new rules of copyright. It also lists over 2,500 markets.

Burnett, Hallie, and Whit. *Fiction Writer's Handbook*, New York: Barnes and Noble, 1975. Don't miss this one if you are serious about writing fiction. These two writers will teach you everything you wanted to know about writing stories—and more. They supply you with illustrations from the works of well-known writers, past and present.

Duncan, Lois. *How to Write and Sell Your Personal Experiences*, Cincinnati: Writer's Digest Books, 1979. This is the book that will teach you how to capitalize on a great source for writing fact and fiction—you!

Fitz-Randolph, Jane. *How to Write for Children and Young Adults*, New York: Harper and Row, 1979. This book will tell you what to write, how to write it, and where to sell it if you are interested in the juvenile field. An unusual aspect of this guide is the section devoted to plays, motion pictures, and TV scripts.

Hilton, Suzanne. *Who Do You Think You Are?* New York: The New American Library, Inc., 1976. This is the guide that will show you how to find out about your family tree. Step by step it points out how to dig up your roots and how to organize them. An added bonus: The author tells how Alex Haley did his research.

Hull, Helen (ed.). *The Writer's Book,* New York: Barnes and Noble, 1965. This is a down-to-earth, practical guide to writing every kind of fiction and nonfiction with advice from professional men and women who have polished their craft to a fine degree.

Krantz, Judith. "A Few Words to a Beginning Writer," *The Writer,* December, 1980. This fiction writer lists twelve rules for becoming a selling writer and uses her own experiences to emphasize her points. You'll learn that it is important to outline, work regular hours, find your own style, choose the right area in which to work, etc.

Manners, William. *Wake Up and Write,* New York: Arco, 1977. Here's a book that will inspire you to sit down and write. The author goes one step farther: He'll give you the incentive to write prolifically even in your spare time. Mr. Manner's writing is informal and enthusiastic, and yet contains basic information.

Neff, Glenda Tennant (ed.) *1988 Writer's Market,* Cincinnati: Writer's Digest Books, 1987. This book tells you how to write that creative query letter, what rights to ask for, how much to charge for certain freelance jobs, etc. It also provides you with a list of 4,000 markets for all categories of writing.

Zinsser, William. *On Writing Well,* New York: Harper and Row, 1980. If nonfiction is your field, this informal guide is for you. The author believes that a writer can achieve his greatest strength with the least clutter, so be prepared for cutting out unnecessary words from your manuscripts. Critics maintain that this book should be placed on your shelf next to *The Elements of Style.*

Index

t

u

About the Author

Peggy Teeters's worldwide travels as an army wife have provided the backgrounds for her many published stories, columns, articles, books, and TV and radio scripts. She has spent two years as a writer/broadcaster of a weekly radio show in Berlin; thirteen years as a women's columnist for her local newspaper; and eighteen years as a teacher of beginning writing courses in an adult education program near her home in Virginia. Her experience in all these areas was the source of inspiration for this book.

Other Books of Interest

General Writing Books

Beginning Writer's Answer Book, edited by Kirk Polking (paper) $12.95

Getting the Words Right: How to Revise, Edit and Rewrite, by Theodore A. Rees Cheney $14.95

How to Increase Your Word Power, by the editors of Reader's Digest $19.95

How to Write a Book Proposal, by Michael Larsen $9.95

Pinckert's Practical Grammar, by Robert C. Pinckert $14.95

The 29 Most Common Writing Mistakes & How to Avoid Them, by Judy Delton $9.95

The Writer's Digest Guide to Manuscript Formats, by Buchman & Groves $16.95

Writer's Guide to Research, by Lois Horowitz $9.95

Writer's Market, edited by Glenda Neff $21.95

Nonfiction Writing

Basic Magazine Writing, by Barbara Kevles $16.95

How to Sell Every Magazine Article You Write, by Lisa Collier Cool $14.95

How to Write & Sell the 8 Easiest Article Types, by Helene Schellenberg Barnhart $14.95

Writing Nonfiction that Sells, by Samm Sinclair Baker $14.95

Fiction Writing

Creating Short Fiction, by Damon Knight (paper) $8.95

Fiction Writer's Market, edited by Laurie Henry $18.95

Handbook of Short Story Writing, by Dickson and Smythe (paper) $8.95

How to Write & Sell Your First Novel, by Oscar Collier with Frances Spatz Leighton $14.95

Writing the Modern Mystery, by Barbara Norville $15.95

Writing the Novel: From Plot to Print, by Lawrence Block (paper) $8.95

Special Interest Writing Books

The Children's Picture Book: How to Write It, How to Sell It, by Ellen E.M. Roberts (paper) $14.95

The Complete Book of Scriptwriting, by J. Michael Straczynski (paper) $9.95

How to Sell & Re-Sell Your Writing, by Duane Newcomb $10.95

How to Write Tales of Horror, Fantasy & Science Fiction, edited by J.N. Williamson $15.95

How to Write & Sell a Column, by Raskin & Males $10.95

How to Write & Sell Your Personal Experiences, by Lois Duncan (paper) $9.95

How to Write the Story of Your Life, by Frank P. Thomas $14.95

Writing Short Stories for Young People, by George Edward Stanley $15.95

The Writing Business

A Beginner's Guide to Getting Published, edited by Kirk Polking $10.95

How to Write Irresistible Query Letters, by Lisa Collier Cool $10.95

How You Can Make $25,000 a Year Writing (No Matter Where You Live), by Nancy Edmonds Hanson $15.95

Literary Agents: How to Get & Work with the Right One for You, by Michael Larsen $9.95

Professional Etiquette for Writers, by William Brohaugh $9.95

To order directly from the publisher, include $2.00 postage and handling for 1 book and 50¢ for each additional book. Allow 30 days for delivery.

Writer's Digest Books, Dept. B, 1507 Dana Avenue, Cincinnati, Ohio 45207

Credit card orders call TOLL-FREE

1-800-543-4644 (Outside Ohio)

1-800-551-0884 (Ohio only)

Prices subject to change without notice.